The Lesson of the Lost Horse:
A Chinese-American Journey of Hope and Love
A Memoir

by

Joanna Ng
吳潤冰

TELEMACHUS PRESS

THE LESSON OF THE LOST HORSE: A CHINESE-AMERICAN JOURNEY OF HOPE AND LOVE A MEMOIR

Cover design by Telemachus Press, LLC

Cover Art:
Copyright © Thinkstock/93863854/Hemera
Copyright © iStockphoto/10323751

Published by Telemachus Press, LLC
http://www.telemachuspress.com

ISBN# 978-1-938701-41-2 (eBook)
ISBN# 978-1-938701-85-6 (paperback)

Version 2013.02.09

Printed in the United States of America

10 9 8 7 6 5 4 3 2 1

AUTHOR'S NOTE

All the characters in this book are real. I have changed some of the names either by request of the person or because I feel that I need to protect his/her privacy.

Dedicated to the memory of my parents

For Ryan and Megan
And for Clark

Contents

The Lesson of the Lost Horse:
A Chinese-American Journey of Hope and Love
A Memoir

1

The Old Farmer Who Lost His horse

塞翁失馬

The Chinese fable about the illusiveness of fortunes
(Or how bad fortune turns out for the best)

LONG AGO, IN a faraway land near the frontier, there lived an old farmer. One dark stormy night he found his horse missing. It was said that the horse was seen running outside the border of the country. Upon hearing the news, the neighbors came to comfort him for the unfortunate loss. "Such bad luck," they said sympathetically.

But the old man was unperturbed. "It's all right. Unfortunate things happen. It'll turn out okay."

One night the old man heard noises outside his house. When he went outside to check on the commotion, to his surprise he saw that his horse had returned, bringing with him another beautiful horse.

"Congratulations on your good fortune," the neighbors cheered. "What a stroke of luck to have your horse back and a bonus horse on top of it!"

The old farmer was subdued and reflective. "I got a new horse for nothing. It's hard to say whether it is good or bad. We'll see."

The son of the old man was very fond of the new horse, but the horse needed to be tamed. One day, while trying to break in the wild horse, he was thrown and broke his legs. The injury was so serious that he would never walk again. The neighbors came to offer their condolences. "Don't fret," the farmer said. "Maybe some good will come of this."

A year later, the war broke out. Military officials came to the village to draft young men into the army. Seeing that the farmer's son was crippled, they passed him up. It was a bad war, and many of the youths who were recruited died in the war. The farmer's son was spared.

2

What Happens Now?

WHEN I STEP out of the plane into the cool early morning San Francisco air, I know I won't be able to go home again, at least not any time soon.

I have just thrown up on the plane. For the first time ever, I tried a taste of red wine. I found out I had no tolerance for alcohol; it's an Asian thing, some kind of missing enzyme issue. The wine was offered and it was free. I thought I should celebrate my big adventure of coming to America. Over twenty hours on the plane, plus a layover somewhere to refuel, didn't help. Fatigue, jet lag, and cheap wine were not a good mix.

I felt a twinge of envy in my stomach as I watched Magdalen, my travel companion and childhood friend, being met by her family at the San Francisco airport. I don't know when I will see my friend again. She was more than generous. On the plane, she had given me twenty dollars for my Smith-Corona portable typewriter. She didn't need the typewriter but she knew I needed the money. I have only seventy dollars in my pocket, and I know nobody in the States. She has relatives in California and in Boston, where she will be going to school. She knew I needed the money more than she did.

Before I stepped out of the plane, I had changed into my Sunday best—a black and white hounds-tooth suit with a short skirt, pale stockings, and black leather shoes. I want to properly present myself to my new country. In my steel suitcase I carry all the possessions I have amassed during the two years I worked as a teacher in Hong Kong: my best clothes, a beloved blanket, a dictionary, and the one and only portrait of my family. Among my prized possessions is a single place setting of western-style flatware—a fork, a spoon, and a knife. I had gone into one of the huge department stores that had just opened up in Hong Kong. Many times I had looked into the windows and wondered if I could ever afford to buy anything in there. Going to America was the perfect excuse to walk into the store. Buying the flatware was exciting. I am going to a western country. Americans don't use chopsticks; this much I know.

But what do I really know about western life? I have never stepped outside Macau and Hong Kong. I don't know anything about America except for the handful of American movies I have seen. *The Ten Commandments*, *The Bridge on the River Kwai*, and *The Sound of Music*—a few of the American movies I remember seeing—told me nothing about Americans or what life would be like in America. The thought of living among foreigners petrifies me. I am too shy and timid. I can hardly look a stranger in the eye. How will I cope with a whole world of *Gweilos* (foreign devils)?

Chicago, where I'm headed, doesn't sound like a warm and fuzzy place, either. I have heard that the weather is cold and that gangsters live there. What will happen when I get to Chicago? I don't know a single person there. All I have in my wallet was the address of Barat College, the school I have come to attend, and one phone number—that of a friend of a friend of my sister Amy.

Amy wants me to go to England. She went there with her fiancé Fred three years ago. She is working to put herself through law school. Although there is some financial support from Fred's family, I know she is just getting by. Amy tells me I could come to England to be a nurse. She is confident that I could support myself on a nurse's stipend and that she could even find me a lawyer husband. But Amy doesn't understand. I can't go to England. I can't stand to live in the shadow of my gifted and pretty sister. I have to make my own way, even if it kills me.

Here I am, trying to "show them" again, only this time I have gone too far. I have always been too proud, not needing anyone's help. Leaving home and going off to a faraway country that I know next to nothing about seemed like a good idea six months ago, but now it scares me. Am I being brave, or am I just naïve and reckless? In the short span of years that I have lived so far, I always had a plan; but this time, I am just winging it.

I left behind what is considered a good job in Hong Kong. I had built a respectable reputation as a fourth-grade teacher at True Light Middle School. My students adored me. The pay was decent by Hong Kong standards. Never mind that I hated the job and felt that my life was a prison sentence. I was only seventeen when I took the job. (At that time, only a high school diploma was needed to teach in Hong Kong.) What do I know about job satisfaction? How could I know what I really want in life? I am not sure, but I *do* know that I don't want to be a schoolteacher any more.

I can only imagine how my mother must have felt when she came to see me off at the airport. She was the only one who could come. My father had to stay home to take care of the store. We ran into a classmate at the airport. The two mothers talked. It was a welcome relief to make small talk with another mother so nobody would start to cry; at any time now, the floodgates would open and the tears would pour. I wanted to hug my mother, but Chinese don't hug. She kept telling me over and over again to take care of myself. I told her repeatedly not to worry. As I walked through the boarding gate, I kept turning back to look at her. I knew she would be standing by the window of the boarding terminal until the plane took off. I knew she wouldn't leave even after the plane had disappeared into the clouds.

I had pleaded with my parents to let me go even though we had absolutely no friends or family in America. They had worried and fretted. How would they know if I was all right? Who would they call? How would they call? To make an international call they would have to go to the post office. It's very expensive, but that isn't even the point. I have no personal contact information to leave with them except my school address. It's a huge leap of faith to let your nineteen-year-old daughter go off to a foreign country that you know nothing about.

I understand now. It was an act of love—amazing, unselfish love. My parents are poor. They have no money to give me. The only thing they could give me is their sacrifice to let me go. They know I want an education. They know I want to make my own destiny. They know I don't want to be stuck in Hong Kong with only the prospect of a marriage proposal that would guarantee a conventional life that I don't want. They are barely eking out a living with their small coffee business. Times in Macau in 1969 were extremely hard. I still had three brothers left at home. They would need every ounce of my parents' resources to help them find their future as well.

After clearing customs, I ask for directions to my final destination—Chicago. I barely manage with my stilted English, but I find out that I need to go to a different terminal, the domestic terminal. The walk from the international terminal to the domestic terminal seems unbearably long. The sun is shining with a welcoming glow, yet I am trembling in the 60-degree temperature of the California morning. My heart aches with a thousand emotions.

I have arrived in America. All I could think was: *what happens now?*

Part One

The Horse from the Countryside:
Lessons from my Childhood

3

Macau

MACAU IS RAINING money. The government sends its residents a 7000 Macau Patacas check (worth about $800 U.S.) every year. The Macau government's coffers are overflowing, so it shares its good fortunes with its citizens. Three years ago in 2009, Macau overtook the Las Vegas strip as the world's No. 1 gaming revenue market. This year it looks like it will earn five times more than Las Vegas. When you see the glitzy lights of the Venetian, the Wynn, the MGM, you'd think you've landed on the strip itself. But when you see the faces of the patrons and the Chinese characters written on the marquee signs, you know you're not in Nevada. The Chinese believe in luck. Gambling is big in this part of the world. Gambling has propelled Macau to the top of the gaming industry in the past thirty years. Few people know the Macau in which I grew up.

The Macau that I knew was a poor Portuguese colony. The Portuguese first set foot in Macau in the early sixteenth century and were instrumental in establishing Macau as a trading center between China and Europe. Beginning in 1670, Portugal leased the territory, although there was no transfer of sovereignty. The Portuguese ruled Macau until it was handed back to China in 1999.

Macau's fortunes changed in the nineteenth century when the British settled in Hong Kong. Hong Kong's deep waters attracted ships and international trade, and Hong Kong soon became one of the world's major commercial centers. Macau's importance quickly declined.

During the time I was growing up, Macau was poor and sleepy. Imagine an entire economy sustained by hand-made joss sticks (incense) and firecrackers. Later plastic flowers, then textiles and garments, toys, electronics, and footwear replaced them. The economy of Macau took a huge turn when gambling came to Macau in the early 1970s. Greyhound racing, Jai Lai, and later the casinos came to Macau, transforming the city from an impoverished small town into a buzzing metropolis. Prosperity is a double-edged sword. Gambling brought money and jobs into Macau, but with it, the quiet charm of old Macau disappeared into the history books forever.

Macau in the 1950s was a tiny little island with an eclectic mix of sun-washed Portuguese and Chinese style buildings, funny Portuguese street names, and quaint cobblestone streets. Western European colonial-style structures stood in stark contrast to stylistic Buddhist temples and other ancient buildings. Everywhere there were signs of its colonial and missionary past—the Mount Fortress, the Ruins of St. Paul, and the Senado Square—all reminders of a history of Portuguese rule that was marked by the influence of the British, Manchu, Mandarins, and European traders in this tiny territory.

Where is Macau? Macau lies on the western side of the Pearl River Delta across from Hong Kong to the east, bordering Guangdong province to the north, and facing the South China Sea to the east and south. The city is small, just eleven square miles. The old streets of Macau were narrow, winding, and twisting, as the city was built for pedestrians only. Macau could have been mistaken for a small village in Portugal, except when you saw the people who lived there.

Over ninety-five percent of Macau's population was Chinese, specifically, Cantonese from the southern part of China, mostly from the Guangdong province. My grandfather was born in the Nanhai District in present-day Guangzhou, known historically as Canton. Cantonese is one of the major dialects of spoken Chinese, with over 70 million speakers. Today you will find Cantonese in the native areas of Guangdong and Guangxi, and in Hong Kong, Macau, Singapore, Malaysia, and Indonesia.

Being Cantonese is more than just speaking a different dialect. It is a different culture. Cantonese love to eat, and our cuisine is among the best. Cantonese cuisine is characterized by its variety of cooking methods, freshness, and use of seafood. Dim sum, the delectable breakfast finger foods, is the most famous Cantonese invention. Roast duck, suckling pig, barbeque pork, chicken feet, and all things sweet-and-sour are just a few examples of the delicious cuisine that came out of Canton.

Cantonese like to greet each other with "Have you had your meal yet?" This is the same as saying, "Hi, how are you?" It goes to show the importance that food plays in the Cantonese culture.

Cantonese are loud. We exaggerate with our facial expressions and gesture with our fingers. The tone of our dialect is high pitched and brusque. Non-Cantonese just think that we are being rude and argumentative. The Cantonese dialect is difficult to learn. It has nine tones, whereas Mandarin has only four. Worse yet, the Cantonese dialect has its own grammatical structure that is completely different from Mandarin, which means that Cantonese children get the short end of the stick—they have to learn to speak in Cantonese and write in Mandarin!

So I was born Cantonese. I love to eat, I am loud, and I tend to get very animated when I talk. Even as I become more multicultural, the Cantonese in me is unmistakable.

The street where I was born was called Green Grass Street. Funny thing is, when I was born in 1949, there was no grass, only a dusty semi-paved cobblestone road. The street was narrow. Dimly lit ma-and-pa stores lined both sides of the street. I recall a grocer, a wine shop, and a candy store. There was an old temple and a flight of stone stairs at the end of the street.

The house where I was born was a two-story structure housing my father's restaurant *Tin Heng* on the ground floor and our living quarters on the second floor. There was a working well right in the middle of the building. I remember accidentally dropping something valuable into the well. Later, indoor plumbing came into the house and the well was covered up so that two bedrooms could be built for my four siblings and me. My brothers had the first floor, right next to the bathroom, with a window that opened into the bathroom for light. My sister and I shared the floor above where the ceiling was very low and a steel beam ran through the middle of it. My bed was right under the beam. I can't tell you how many times I hit my head because I got up too fast and forgot that the beam was right there. It's a wonder I didn't suffer permanent brain damage from hitting my head so many times!

The name of my father's restaurant *Tin Heng* **(天香)** stood for "Heavenly Fragrance" or "Sweet-smelling Skies"—both rather romantic names befitting its rural setting. The rustic Portuguese colony had no cars, no television, and no modern conveniences of any kind to speak of. In the early days when we owned the restaurant, we had many livestock at the back of our building. There were pigs, chickens, rabbits, and even monkeys at one time, plus a couple of dogs and many stray cats. We picked eggs that were freshly laid and still warm. My mother sold them to a woman who came for them every morning. She had a tool that measured the size of the eggs, which determined the price they would fetch. The chicks and bunnies were adorable, but we learned from a very young age not to get too attached as they might end up on the dinner table the next day. I even witnessed a mother pig giving birth one night. There was such commotion. They kept coming, those little pink piglets. I didn't realize at that time this was where suckling roast pigs came from.

So it was in this setting of a rural, unaffected, simple way of life that I was born and raised. Nothing in my childhood prepared me for the life that waited for me. Everything in my childhood shaped the future upon which I was about to embark.

4

Different Worlds

"IF DOORS SHOULD match, so should the families."
"門當戶對"

This is the Chinese saying about what constitutes a proper match. The saying touts the importance of compatibility in a successful marriage. A proper match is not just a match between families of equal wealth and status, but also educational level, values, culture, and so on.

My parents came from two very different worlds. The difference in their family backgrounds was responsible for much of the turmoil in their marriage.

My mother was born to a middle class family in Hong Kong and raised with a refined upbringing. The second child of four, she was the only daughter. My maternal grandfather was a progressive, educated man. He worked for the Union Insurance Society of Canton, a local insurance company with its parent company in the United Kingdom, and made a good living earning both a salary and a commission as one of their officers. He was a devoted Christian who served as a member of the Church Council in his local church. My memory of him was that of an elegant, soft-spoken, kindly man with snow-white hair who always dressed in western style clothes. My maternal grandparents were married in an arranged marriage, but it was a happy marriage. True to the self-deprecating ways of Chinese women in her day, my grandmother saw herself as plain and unattractive, and she couldn't understand why my grandfather was devoted to her. But I know my grandfather saw her differently. My grandmother was poised and smart, and the love of my grandfather's life.

As a young girl, my mother attended the prestigious Belilios Public School (BPS). Founded in 1890, BPS was the first government school for girls in Hong Kong. It was also one of the first bilingual schools, so my mother learned English at an early age. Besides achieving a high academic standard, the school also promoted development in the arts, music, and sports. My mother was an accomplished swimmer and won many awards in swimming competitions.

My maternal grandparents had high expectations for their children, all of whom went to prestigious schools with the toughest admission requirements in Hong Kong. I heard stories from my mother about how her brothers were disciplined for their academic failures. When they did not achieve the desired grades, they had to stay up all night to reflect on their failures. The disciplinary tactics apparently worked. Her brothers all went to college, which was a remarkable accomplishment for children of that era. Two of my uncles went to England where they attained advanced degrees. All three became successful professionals: an architect, a medical doctor, and an engineering professor. My mother always thought she would go to college when she grew up.

My maternal grandfather doted on my mother. My uncle once told me that my mother "was the pearl on my grandfather's palm," a Chinese saying similar to the expression "the apple of his eye." She was the quintessential Chinese daughter—sweet, obedient, helpful and thoughtful, which made her the darling of her father. Every evening she listened at the door for my grandfather's footsteps, and as soon as he was at the door, she ran to him with his slippers. Then she would pull up her stool and sit by his armchair while he drank his tea and read the newspaper. At the dinner table, she would patiently wait for my grandfather to give her the choice helpings. Her brothers, however, often got smacked on their chopsticks by their father to stop them from grabbing the best morsels of the evening meal.

My mother was sixteen when her family came to Macau to flee the bombing of Hong Kong during the Second World War. Her family rented an apartment across from my father's family home. They met as neighbors and soon fell in love. My father was tall and handsome, smart and confident. My mother had attended all-girls schools all her life had never yet dated a boy. She fell head over heels in love with my father. When the war was over, my father asked my grandfather for my mother's hand in marriage. They were married in a traditional Chinese ceremony at age twenty. Soon afterward, my mother's family moved back to Hong Kong. My mother would soon lead a very different life from the one she had planned.

My father's upbringing couldn't have been more different from my mother's. He was born into a very old-world Chinese family as the third child and the second son of the first wife. My grandfather had three wives. It was an acceptable practice in China for men of his generation to have more than one wife if they were financially capable. In fact, being able to afford a large family with multiple wives was a status symbol. My grandmother was the first wife, the wife with the highest standing and the only legal wife. Unfortunately, she died at a very young age and left behind four children: a daughter and three sons. My father lost his mother to cancer at the tender age of nine. I grew up listening to my father's stories of feeding opium to his mother on what was called the "opium bed." Opium was the only pain medication available at the time. How horrible it must have been for a young boy of nine to watch his mother die! My grandfather subsequently had two more wives who bore him more children. Naturally, these other wives favored their own. My father had to fend for himself and his younger brother after their mother died. In a large Chinese family where generations live together and the adults are focused on making a living, there is very little room for love and nurturing, especially if your own mother isn't there to look after you.

My paternal grandfather moved to Macau from China as a young man. He made his money as a businessman who barely knew how to write his name and use the abacus. He was a hot tempered, opinionated man who didn't believe in education, so he didn't spend a lot of money on the education of his children. My father, however, was ambitious and hard working. He was a very proud man who tried all his life to prove that he was smarter than his peers and better than his circumstances. To my father's way of thinking, success was measured by being able to make money—lots of money. Unfortunately, the fates didn't smile on him. My father died without knowing the financial success he had dreamed of achieving. The most poignant remark I heard my father make one time in his later years was "The biggest regret in my life is that I never struck it rich."

Before my grandfather separated the households, the whole Ng family lived under one roof. The members of the Ng household included my grandfather, his two wives, their eleven children, many grandchildren, cooks, maids, and other domestics. I was a baby then, but I have some sketchy memories of the big, bustling household. We took up an entire street block of four apartments on Green Grass Street. My grandfather owned several shops and restaurants, which were on the first floor. The family lived on the second floor. The four upstairs apartments were actually one large living space connected by doors and hallways.

Because my grandmother died when my father was very young, I grew up with the second and third grandmothers, whom we called Ma Ma and Sum Ma respectively. Let me tell you, more wasn't better. There was a lot of bickering between Ma Ma and Sum Ma. The yelling and screaming from across the balconies could often be heard by the whole neighborhood. Since each wife was younger than the one preceding her, some of my uncles and aunts were younger than I was. It was strange to call a three-year-old "uncle."

When my mother entered the Ng household, she was the second of two daughters-in-law as my father was the second son to get married. Daughters-in-law had very low status in those days. They were just one-step above servants. Mothers-in-law who had suffered harsh treatment when they were daughters-in-law were bent on avenging their suffering on the next generation. My mother had to do all of my father's laundry even though there were plenty of servants. She had to get up at six o'clock every morning to offer tea to her mothers-in-law. She had to manage all the expenses of her husband and her children on one small monthly allowance.

Dinner in a big traditional Chinese household was a study in societal hierarchy. Dinner for the adults was served in the main dining room. Seated around the huge, round mahogany table were my grandfather, my grandmothers, the children (my father and his siblings), various elderly uncles and aunts, and then the daughters-in-law. The best dishes of meat and poultry were placed in front of the most senior family members. The lowly dishes of beans and vegetables were placed at the far end where the daughters-in-law sat. At the first indication that one of the elders needed a refill of rice or a fresh cup of tea, the daughters-in-law dropped their chopsticks to fulfill the request. Throughout the course of the meal, the daughters-in-law had to get up from the table so many times that they were lucky to have eaten anything at all. In her days as a newlywed daughter-in-law, my mother weighed less than ninety pounds.

My mother's westernized, progressive upbringing played out in sharp contrast against my father's traditional, archaic Chinese upbringing. The clash of the two worlds contributed to my parents' tumultuous marriage. It accounted for a great deal of the misery that my mother suffered. My mother once said to me, "This is the life I have chosen," as if resigned to the saying, "I made my bed, so I must lie in it." This victim mentality shaped my mother's personality. It almost shaped mine, as I was so much like my mother.

Many Chinese books and movies have told the unhappy stories of old-world Chinese women born into a life of misery and hardship. It was an era when Chinese women had very low status and very few options. Deep-rooted culture and traditions shaped their lives. Many turned to religion and superstition because they had so little power over their happiness and their fate. As it was with my mother, fear, despair, and bitterness soon swallowed their personalities and smothered their dreams.

My story could have been the same. I had no other role models but my mother and the self-sacrificing, unhappy lives of thousands of women in Chinese history. Like them, I wasn't taught to dream.

5
Two Names, Three Birthdays, Four Siblings

I HAVE A name that wasn't given by my parents. I have a recorded birth date that is faked. I am a twin on paper but not in real life. All these should make me a pretty messed-up person, but they are just the facts of my life. Many people in my time and circumstance have stories like this.

I was given the Chinese name *Ng Yuen Bing* (吳潤冰) when I was born. *Bing* literally translated, means *ice*. Contrary to what the word suggests—that of being cold and indifferent—Bing is a very feminine Chinese name and it means, "Clear as ice." There is a Chinese saying that expands on this idea: "Bing Xue Chong Ming," which translates into "as bright and intelligent as the ice and snow." Well, some phrases just don't translate well. I'd like to think, however, that my parents meant for me to be the smart one.

When I was in fourth grade, my mother enrolled me in a Catholic school run by nuns from the Sacred Heart Canossian order. Public schools in Macau were considered very substandard at the time. All the better schools were privately run, and those run by the Catholic Church were deemed the best. Shortly after I started fourth grade at Sacred Heart College, all of us were told to go home and get ourselves an English name. The reason—the nuns, most of whom came from Italy, were having a hard time with our Chinese names. My mother didn't know many western names. She decided to name me Elizabeth, after the beautiful American actress Elizabeth Taylor. But it was not to be. When my turn came to tell the teacher my new name, she shook her head and pointed to a girl seated in the front.

"No, no, no. She is Elizabeth. I can't have two Elizabeths in my class."

She thought about it for two seconds, and then she told me emphatically. "Your name is Joanna. J-O-A-N-N-A. Write it down and tell your mother." All the way home, I practiced saying my name so that I could tell my mother. That was how I got my name—from a Catholic nun when I was in the fourth grade.

For someone who was supposed to be an Elizabeth but became a Joanna, I give new meaning to the definition of "identity crisis" when I tell people I also have three birthdays.

I was born on July 21 on the lunar calendar. Thus, my Chinese birthday is July 21. However, the lunar calendar is not perfectly synchronized with the western calendar, and lunar July 21 fell on western September 13 in the year of my birth. Thus, September 13 is also my birthday. Yet my legal birthday is neither July 21 nor September 13. It is November 21. Here is the story of my legal birthday.

When I was fourteen, the Portuguese government decided that everyone must get a birth certificate. Up until then, most of the people living in Macau didn't have any official papers. All of us were born at home so there were no legal records of our births. To get a birth certificate, all that was needed were two witnesses and the payment of a registration fee. The fee structure was two-tiered, one rate for adults, and another for children. The fee for children (fourteen and under) was substantially less than that of an adult.

My parents needed to get birth certificates for the five of us. They decided that my brother Charlie and I were close enough in age (we are sixteen months apart) that they could pass us off as twins. This way they would only have to pay one fee. They would save even more money if we were under fourteen. So they picked a birth date that would put us just under fourteen. An arbitrary date, November 21, became our birth date. That is the official birth date that Charlie and I have on our birth certificates.

So, for the savings of less than fifty dollars, I got a fake birth date for life. It is the date written on my birth certificate, passport, driver's license, and on every piece of legal paperwork I own. It would be the date to usher in my Social Security payments. It was the only birthday that my children knew for years. With the passage of time, my mother could no longer remember my real birth date. She sent me birthday cards on November 21.

Having a name given by a nun and a made-up birth date didn't have a huge impact on me. But being a middle child did.

There were five children in my family. By birth order, I am right smack in the middle as child number three. My sister Amy was the oldest, followed by my brother Charlie. After me, there were two more boys, Jack and Jimmy. My mother used to say that the five of us were like the five fingers of her hand: all part of the same hand but each one very different from the others. She was right; we couldn't be more different.

Amy's Chinese name is *Yuen Tong*, which was chosen by my uncle, my father's older brother. My uncle was the oldest male and had the right to name my father's first-born—another Chinese tradition. *Tong* means *Autumn Begonia*—a famous Chinese flower. In school, Amy took my mother's English name, which was also Amy.

Amy exemplified the typical first-born. She was sensible, matter-of-fact, practical, and always in control. She was a pragmatist who didn't allow emotions to rule her decisions. Amy liked her life well planned and orderly. She excelled in school and repeatedly earned top honors in her class. She was the first to leave home to strike out on her own, setting the standard for all of us to follow. She chose to work in the legal field, which suited her personality, and she built a successful career as a corporate lawyer, eventually rising to senior partnership in a large law firm in Hong Kong. Amy's life worked out just the way she had planned it.

My brother Charlie was two years younger than Amy and one year older than I was. His name was *Chi-Shun*. *Shun* means *meek and docile*. I think his name was intended to connote decency, affability, and goodness. The Bible says, "Blessed are the meek, for they shall inherit the earth." His name may work very well in the biblical sense, but in practical life, it didn't serve my brother well. Charlie was generous and trusting, but sometimes naïve in his interactions with the world around him. Academically he couldn't compare to Amy, who set the bar very high. Because of that, he got more than his share of scolding and punishment, which greatly affected his self-esteem.

In my parents' defense, they didn't know any better. That was the way Chinese children were raised in those days (and some still are). Parents were supposed to motivate by negative encouragement. They told their children they were stupid as a way of motivating them to do better. It didn't always work. In some cases, it inflicted permanent damage. My brother Charlie was by no means stupid. He had a sunny and optimistic disposition and he worked hard. After I left for America, Charlie joined Amy in England where he completed his studies and went on to become a Chartered Accountant.

My brother Jack was two and half years younger than I was. Fourth in the line-up, he was the baby until my youngest brother Jimmy came along. Jack's Chinese name is *Chi-Fung*. *Fung* means *razor-sharp*. The word can also be translated *a pioneer*. Jack was named by my mother. His name foretold his accomplishments later in life.

Jack was my only sibling who never left home. He started with very humble beginnings working in the docks of the Hong Kong harbor. When the casinos came to Macau, Jack caught his first break as a Blackjack dealer. From that point on, there was no stopping Jack. His smarts, integrity, and work ethic took him to one of the highest ranks in the business. Eventually he became the general manager of one of the newest casinos in Macau. Jack was completely self-taught. He was also a self-starter with business interests that ranged from real estate to French wine to chocolates. Jack exemplified the word *entrepreneur*.

My youngest brother Jimmy was born nine years after Jack. His Chinese name is *Chi-Mei*. Phonetically, *Mei* sounds the same as the Chinese word for *last*. My mother was determined that he would be the last child born to the family because at the time of Jimmy's birth, my parents' financial situation was so bad that it was unthinkable to bring another child into the world. My mother wasn't alone in thinking this. Poverty in Macau at the time when Jimmy was born had reached epidemic heights. Many families chose to abort rather than add another mouth to feed.

Jimmy would tell you that he was the last in everything in the family, especially the last to know what was going on. Because of the age difference between him and us, he grew up very much as an only child, but he tried so hard to keep up with the rest of us. In spite of his size, he could beat any of us in a game of table tennis. His personality was happy-go-lucky, and he was a consummate jokester. It was his way of getting attention.

Jimmy's calling was electrical engineering, and he excelled in the field of wireless communications. Jimmy always seemed to know what was important in life. He eventually left his high-stress, high-paying job in Chicago and moved his family to sunny California. Today he is happily settled in a beautiful family home along the hillside of San Diego. You see, *Mei* also means *beautiful*. Life is beautiful for my brother Jimmy.

I was very different from any of my siblings. I was the third child and the "redundant daughter." My parents already had a son and a daughter before I came along. Comparisons between my older sister and me were inevitable. Amy got all the attention being the first-born and the first to do everything, whereas I mainly stayed in the shadows. I felt invisible.

As a child, I was shy and brooding. My baby pictures show a chubby child with her hair cut short, looking like a boy. My clothes were mostly hand-me-downs from my sister Amy. Growing up I kept to myself and had few friends. I preferred to spend my time studying, reading, or listening to music. In school, I was not good in sports and athletics. In fact, I always thought of myself as a complete klutz. I even cracked my two front teeth learning to jump rope!

There was a yearning in me to show the world that I was special. When I didn't receive the attention I craved from my parents, I became increasingly sensitive. At their slightest negative remark, I would go to my room and slam the door. Then I would lie on my bed and for the one-hundredth time, I would fantasize about how I would one day show them what I was capable of accomplishing. In my fantasy, I saw myself leaving home and becoming outrageously rich and successful. Then, I would come home to show off my success, driving up to the house in my fancy car. Everyone would come out to see who this important person was. My parents and my siblings would be so sorry that they had mistreated me. They would be begging for my forgiveness. What do you do with fantasies like that?

All my life I worked very hard to make up for what I thought I lacked. I worked very hard in school. I worked very hard at my job. I worked very hard to be a good daughter, a good mother, a good wife. I was a consummate perfectionist. When my mind took hold of something, it would not let go until I had accomplished what I set out to do. If I really wanted something in life, no obstacle was ever too big. I would find a way to attain it. I had the determination of steel.

Among my siblings, I was closest to Charlie as we were only one year apart in age. Charlie and I played the "Game of Fighting Animals" (a board game) together. We walked to and from school together. We went to movies together. To save money, we would buy one ticket and squeeze ourselves into a single seat because movie tickets were purchased per seat, not per person. My fondest memory of Charlie and me was watching *Ben-Hur* sharing a seat and a banana.

That is not to say that Charlie and I always got along. We had such different personalities and temperaments. I was conscientious and uptight. Charlie was laid-back and happy-go-lucky. Even though I was the younger sister, I was responsible for Charlie in our daily routines. Everyday I had the chore of making sure Charlie got home from school without loitering. Charlie liked to take his time, stopping every five minutes to pull every tree branch and kick every rock. I was the bossy little sister who could be heard screaming, "Hurry up Charlie or we'll be late again."

Since Jack was my baby brother, I was his protector. Jack was very sweet natured, and I loved playing big sister to him. I was in second grade and Jack was in kindergarten. It could have been Jack's first day of school. My mother couldn't come to pick us up from school and had sent a rickshaw driver. He was crippled in one leg and walked with a bad limp. When Jack saw him, he was scared and started to cry. He clung onto my arm and refused to get on the rickshaw. I assured him that I would not make him get on the rickshaw if he didn't want to. Instead, I walked with him alongside the rickshaw all the way home. The next morning, during the school assembly on the playground, the school principal told of a loving sister who sacrificed her ride to walk with her brother. I was so proud.

I didn't get along with my sister Amy when we were little. There was a period when I couldn't stand the sight of her. I would scowl at her when I saw her in the morning and would tell her to get out of my way. It was irrational. I was angry with her for no good reason. Maybe it was jealousy.

Maybe it was incompatibility. We were so different. Three years apart, we lived in completely different worlds. When she was into school, I was into games. She was into boys when I finally got serious about school. Just as I began to get curious about boys, Amy had left home. I was always one-step behind my sister.

My parents liked to hold Amy up as an example for the rest of us. Hard as I tried, I could never catch up with Amy. Finally, I made up my mind that I didn't want to. I would make my own way. So instead of following Amy to England, I set off for the United States. In the years to come, we were both swept up with careers, marriage, and children while living on two different continents. Years later, we would find each other again. Now that we have grown children of our own, we have come to appreciate each other. Separated by time and distance, it is still a challenge and a work-in-progress to cope with our differences, but I now know that having a sister in my life is a gift.

Jimmy and I had a very different kind of relationship. When I left home, Jimmy was only six years old. I was the big sister who came home with treats and toys for my baby brother so he was always excited to see me. When Jimmy was fifteen, I brought him to the United States to live with me. I was only twenty-six at the time, and I hadn't yet started my own family. For a while, I became his surrogate mother. I attended all of his parent-teacher conferences. I taught him how to drive. He stayed with me until he finished high school. He went to college at the Illinois Institute of Technology (IIT) in downtown Chicago. We enjoyed years of closeness until he moved to California. We were the only family to each other in the United States.

My mother used to say, "When you are children, you belong to one family. When you grow up, you will be separate households." Indeed, for a brief period, only about fifteen years in my case, I grew up together with all my siblings. After that, we were scattered all over the world. There is only one portrait in our family album that shows all of us together—my parents and us five children—and that was taken in 1964, when I was fifteen.

6

Early Childhood Memories

AS WE GREW older, my grandfather's house was bursting at the seams. My grandfather was having more children with his third wife while his grown children were having more children of their own. It was no longer manageable to have all of these growing families under one roof. When I was three years old and shortly after Jack was born, my grandfather decided to separate the family and allow the married children to run their own households and businesses.

My grandfather owned several businesses, so he gave each of his three grown sons one of his restaurants to own and manage. My father got the restaurant *Tin Heng* on Green Grass Street. We moved to the second floor of the restaurant.

Life as a restaurant owner was very hard. My young parents had no experience running a business. Our restaurant was open 365 days a year. Chinese businesses never closed in those days. To stop working would be to stop eating. There were no holidays and no vacations. My mother opened the restaurant at five in the morning and my father closed it at midnight. They were the cook, the waiter, the cashier, and the dishwasher depending on who didn't show up that day. Making money was very difficult, as everyone was poor. There was no accounting system to keep track of the supplies in the back room and theft was rampant. Every customer was on credit. To keep them as customers, my parents had no choice but to allow them to pay at the end of the month. Very few of the accounts were ever paid in full. If they couldn't pay and my parents refused to serve them, they would simply go to the next restaurant and do it all over again. Most restaurants were desperate enough for business that they would gladly extend credit to a new customer.

While my parents were slaving away downstairs in the restaurant, we mostly fended for ourselves upstairs. My father's aunt, whom we called Sum Yi Po or "3rd great aunt," came to live with us. She was the youngest sister of my grandmother who died so young. Sum Yi Po was a pretty young woman who never married. In those days, the only way to escape an arranged marriage was to declare oneself a spinster and enter into service with a family as a maid or nanny. That was what Sum Yi Po did. She took over the household chores for my mother by doing the cooking, the washing, and the cleaning. It was a lot of work, and she didn't get very much pay for it.

My sister was born one year after my parents were married. My brother came two years later and I was born sixteen months after my brother. Between running the restaurant and being constantly ill with childbearing, my mother was overwrought. Amy was sent to live with my maternal grandparents when my brother Charlie was born. Amy had fond memories of the time she spent with my grandparents, who doted on her as the first grandchild on my mother's side of the family. My brother Charlie was the first son born to my parents. In a Chinese family, sons are king; it means the family name will be carried on. My parents hired a nanny to take care of Charlie.

But when I came along there were few options for my care.

My caretaker was an old aunt, a sister of my grandfather, who sold cigarettes outside my parents' restaurant for a living. She had no husband to support her, so she earned a few cents a day selling cigarettes. Her cigarettes were displayed in a wooden tray placed on top of a wooden stand. Camels and Winstons were the brand names I remember. They were sold as individual cigarettes; no one could afford a whole pack. While she waited for customers, she peeled potatoes for my parents' restaurant and watched over me. My earliest childhood memory is of sitting in a wooden high chair, watching her peeling potatoes outside my father's restaurant all day long.

I remember her wrinkled, cheerless face. She had a miserable disposition reflecting her unhappy life. She told grim tales of the horrific things she had suffered during the war. Food was scarce and there was widespread starvation. She recounted gruesome details of how people hunted mice for food, and how they washed the corn from human excretions to eat again. The thought of it grossed me out! Because of her wrenching experiences, she never threw any food away. She was known to hoard food for weeks, even months, until it was green and moldy, and still she ate it. Imagine sitting with her day in and day out, watching her peel potatoes all day long ...

My parents were not strict disciplinarians. They were young parents who really adored their children. By Chinese standards, they were too soft on us. We might have been considered spoiled, even. Aside from schoolwork, we were seldom given any chores. We were never taken to task on anything that I can remember. We had no strict house rules. We were seldom yelled at and almost never physically punished—except this one time.

In every respectable Chinese house, a feather duster hung proudly on the wall. It was the symbol that there was discipline in the household. The feather duster was equivalent to the leather belt. It was the instrument of punishment. The Chinese pride themselves on their eagerness to discipline their children. It shows that they have virtue, that they are good parents. They have the feather duster to prove it.

I was very small, maybe three or four years old. There was a candy store right across the street from our house with jars of tempting treats like sugared plums, candied olives, and dried roasted squid. I had seen my mother's covered dish in her bedroom. It was on top of her dresser. I knew that inside the dish there were coins that could be exchanged for those tasty treats I loved. I remember climbing up using a stool. I got the coins and went across the street. I pointed to the treats I wanted and the nice lady put the change in the front pocket of my coveralls.

Later that day I had to pee. We had no toilets at the time. For the young children's use, a spittoon was placed in a corner of the living room. As I pulled down my coveralls to sit on the spittoon, the coins came tumbling out of my front pocket and scattered onto the living room floor. My parents were stunned. Where did she get the money? What a little thief! She must be punished! From the screaming and yelling, I knew I was in trouble—big trouble. I was ordered to pull up my pants and go into the bedroom where my father was waiting with the feather duster.

I don't remember what happened next. I am sure that I was punished, but I don't remember the beating or the pain. What I do remember is that I was frightened and confused. Why were my parents so angry with me? Had I done something so bad to make my parents punish me? I felt ashamed. They said children understand right from wrong very early on. Perhaps this early incident served to impress on me that money must be earned by hard work and not by taking short cuts. But I am convinced that I was too young to understand.

Despite their young age and inexperience as parents, my parents succeeded in instilling in us strict ethics and moral values. All of us were taught the importance of working hard, of not taking advantage of people and situations, of honor, and of having pride in oneself. These are the same values that I tried very hard to instill in my own children.

The Chinese like to push their children to get an early start in education. So when I was four years old I started kindergarten at a school called Leng Wah School. In the morning I would get dressed and come down to the front of the restaurant where my mother would be sitting behind a counter, cashiering. No matter how hectic the morning or how many waiting customers she had lined up, she would take time to braid my hair into two pigtails and tie ribbons on them. I enjoyed being in the middle of the noise and the chaos, sitting on a stool munching on my breakfast of crusty bun with pork dumplings while my mother worked on my unruly hair.

When I entered grade school, I was transferred to Leng Nam Primary School. It was a renowned Chinese school and the site of the present-day Lou Lim Ieoc Garden. The garden was originally built in the 1900s as the residence of a wealthy local merchant named Lou Kau. Later the fortunes of the family declined and the premise was leased to the Leng Nam Primary School. After I left Macau, the Macau government purchased the site and turned it into a public park in 1974. Today it is regarded as one of the most Chinese of all Chinese gardens and a top tourist destination in Macau.

The site of my grade school was an architectural gem. A towering stone wall surrounded the property. The front gate was a striking ancient Chinese archway. The wealthy Lau Kou family had modeled the grounds after the famous classical Chinese gardens of Soochow. As a result, the property was filled with lotus ponds, winding bridges, whimsical archways, and miniaturized artificial mountains and rock caves. Groves of bamboo and blossoming bushes lined the narrow pathways throughout the estate. Lotus flowers in hues of white and bright pink filled the ponds. A nine-turn bridge zigzagged across the pond to a large classical Chinese pavilion. Stone tables and rock benches provided inviting spots for eating and playing games under shady trees.

My brother Charlie and I share many fond memories of our school days at Leng Nam, as we were only one grade apart. We had endless fun climbing the miniature mountains and crawling through the manmade caves. There were so many hidden paths to explore, so many bridges to run across from one end to the other. The air reverberated with the symphony of chirping birds of all species. The smell of gardenia, hibiscus, and jasmine flowers perfumed the air. It was the magical garden of my childhood.

Everyday my mother came to school to bring us lunch. She carried the hot food in a multi-tiered tin carrier. The stackable containers allowed different dishes to be stored separately in each layer. There was usually a soup, fish or eggs, and always vegetables and rice. We would take our lunch in one of the shady pavilions or around stone tables and stools in the fresh open air. Lunch was the best part of my school day.

I stayed at Leng Nam School until third grade when my mother decided that it was time for me to go to a serious school that taught English. She had the foresight that learning English would play an important role in our future. In spite of the much higher tuition, she decided to enroll me and my sister in the all-girls Catholic school called Sacred Heart College.

When I left Leng Nam School, it marked the end of my Chinese coed non-secular education. It also marked the end of my Shangri-la carefree childhood days. Thinking about eating lunch with my mother sitting in one of the covered outdoor pavilions of my grade school with the rain gently falling on the bamboo trees around us, makes me nostalgic for the old days.

7

Monsoons, Festivals, and the Macau Grand Prix

I WAS BORN and raised in the warm summer haze and stormy rain-drenched days of Portuguese Macau. Even though Macau is a tropical island, it actually has all four seasons. In my memory, I can only recall the extremes—the stifling hot, torrential summers and the frigid cold winters.

Summer is the longest season in Macau, lasting about five months from May to September, with temperatures hovering around 35 °C (95 °F) or higher. Summer in Macau can only be described by two words: hot and steamy. The sky is a constant blue with not a cloud in sight. The obstinate sun hangs transfixed in the midday sky. The humidity is oppressive, engulfing one's body like a blanket of steam. It is the kind of heat that suffocates you. Our clothes were soaked through with perspiration from the minute we woke up until we went to bed. Ten minutes after we took a shower, we needed another one again.

We got very dark in the summer; our skin burned to a deep chocolate brown under the unrelenting sun. Women only went out with umbrellas. It was not fashionable to be dark. Pale, delicate skin was envied as the sign of wealth and refinement, because it meant that you didn't have to be outdoors. Only women who had to work for a living were dark and permanently tanned. How ironic that in the western culture, the reverse is true.

My favorite place to sleep on those hot summer nights was on two wooden planks put on top of two sawhorses in the balcony of our second floor apartment. Here I could catch a breeze if I was lucky. The coolness of the wood planks was a welcome relief to the boiling heat. I would lie there watching the geckos dart around on the ceiling, wondering which one might fall and crawl into my ears while I was sleeping.

We had no refrigerators. Ice trucks delivered huge blocks of ice to the houses and businesses once a day. The ice blocks were then broken into more manageable pieces and used to keep meats and other perishables from spoiling. There was always excitement when the ice truck came. The children would squeal with joy as they watched the men pick up the massive blocks with their ice picks. Everyone ran to catch the splinters of ice flying all over the street.

Macau was cold in the winter, the kind of cold mixed with dampness that chills you to the bone. From January to February the cold air from Siberia passes through Mid China and South China into Macau, bringing with it the cold northerly winds. The temperature sometimes dropped below 10° C and could get as low as the freezing point. There were no fireplaces or heaters. We wore bulky cotton jackets to keep warm. My small hands were so frigid from the cold that it hurt to hold the brushes I used to do my Chinese calligraphy, a required homework every night. Later when I attended Catholic school, we had to wear uniforms. My winter uniform consisted of a thin wool navy blazer and a matching pleated skirt. Underneath the jacket, we wore a white shirt with a navy tie. It was so cold my legs would turn blue. I often wore my uniform to bed on those cold winter nights, so that in the morning I didn't have to change into the stiff icy cold garments. So clever! I thought.

My childhood memories are filled with rainy days in Macau. The humid subtropical climate brought torrential rains. The city had little or no drainage. When it rained heavily, the streets became flooded. The water came knee-high in the narrow streets carrying with it dirt and debris. The floodwater rushed into homes and businesses causing damage and disruption and adding misery to the already challenging daily lives of the Macau people.

While the adults were busy clearing the water off the dirt floors in their buildings, we children were busy making the most of the rain. Our favorite pastime on those rainy days was making paper boats and watching them disappear into the sewage drains. I only knew one way to make a paper boat. It was a simple design and not very sturdy, but it gave me hours of fun.

Better than rainy days were typhoon days. Located to the west of the estuary of Pearl River between mainland China and the South China Sea, Macau has a tropical monsoon climate. The Southwest monsoon blows from April to September, and the Northeast monsoon from September to April. It is during the change of the wind directions that typhoons usually occur.

Those days when the typhoon-warning signal went above 5, schools closed and children stayed home. When the signal went to 8 and above, it was a warning that the center of the typhoon was approaching Macau, and people were advised to take shelter, to reinforce doors and windows, and to listen to the radio for public announcements. In the eye of the typhoon, everything was quiet. Then it poured. The rain came down so hard you thought the sky was falling. *Where did all that water come from?*

And then there's the wind. If you are a small child, you better hang on to something or somebody. The wind can literally pick you up and carry you down the narrow streets of Macau.

In the late summer of 1962, a dramatic incident took place that could have been disastrous for my family. Instead, it became a cherished memory for my siblings and me.

It was a school day, but schools were closed because the typhoon warning signal had gone up to 10, the highest, indicating that a direct hit was imminent. We were running, screaming, and chasing each other around the house much to the exasperation of my mother. She had been mopping the floor all morning because the rain had leaked through the windows. Outside the wind was howling and the rain hammered the roof. In the midst of the howling winds and thundering rain, suddenly there was a loud, crackling noise and the floor shook. We looked up and one of the walls began to develop a huge crack. As we looked on in amazement, the whole wall began to sway. My mother picked up my baby brother Jimmy and we ran for the stairs. We all got out minutes before one entire wall from our second story home fell to the street below. By some miracle, it fell away from the house into the street. No one was hurt—not even the people on the street.

No police or ambulance came. The incident was dramatic but it passed quickly. Hours later, we actually moved back to our second floor home! Our living room was now open to the streets. The people on the street could watch us as if we were on a theater stage. Nobody thought too much of it. Nobody even stopped to stare. People were too engrossed in their daily struggle for survival to pay attention. Life went on.

The typhoon of 1962 was one of the most destructive in the history of the region, killing hundreds and devastating boats and properties. But for me and my siblings, our encounter with fate when the wall fell from our house on that August day became a fond memory in the annals of our childhood.

Our childhood memories are also colored with the sights and sounds of the many Chinese festivals we celebrate throughout the year. Chinese New Year is the most important and colorful Chinese festival. It comes around the end of January or beginning of February and marks the 1st day of the First Moon. It is celebrated for over three days with firecrackers and lion dances on the streets. Crowds visit the temples for New Year blessings. Children don new clothes. Families call on each other and bring New Year treats.

The New Year celebration begins with a family dinner on New Year's Eve. The tradition is similar to Thanksgiving in the United States. Families get together and enjoy a feast of sumptuous traditional food. Roast pork and Chinese sausages are served at the feast. Noodles are eaten for long life. The house is thoroughly cleaned in preparation for the New Year. In more traditional households red stickers are pasted everywhere—over doors and on halls, walls, and food containers. The stickers are printed with words of good fortune, such as *Safe*, *Full*, and *Prosperity* to invoke these blessings for the rest of the year.

My parents would be busy running around to make sure that accounts were settled and employees were paid their bonuses. If you own a business, this is the time when you find out whether you made money that year. For my parents, this was always a tough time of the year. Click. Click. Click. I could see the stress on my mother's face as she poured over the abacus trying to make the numbers work.

My father, on the other hand, loved this time of the year. When all the chores were done and the family dinner was finished, he loved to take us out to the evening flower market and buy a cherry blossom tree to celebrate the New Year. My father loved cherry blossom trees. The beautiful, dainty pink flowers would bloom for days after we took it home and set it in a pot of water. The flowers of spring brought hope for the new year. For my father, it meant the hope of prosperity. Maybe this would be the year that his business would do well. Maybe this would be the year that he would finally make it rich.

My mother made the best New Year treats. Delicious smells filled the house. One of my favorites was a treat called the fried taro nests. Her mother taught her this specialty. Taro, a starchy root vegetable similar to a potato, was cut into thin strips, wound into a loose nest, deep-fried, and then sprinkled with salt. They were salty, crunchy, and addictive, and could be eaten alone or in Chinese congee (rice soup). She also made the best turnip cakes. The radish was shaved into fine strips and mixed with hot rice flour, then seasoned with dried shrimp and scallions, and steamed to a smooth, moist, cake-like perfection.

On the first day of the New Year, we were awakened by the loud sound of firecrackers very early in the morning. It was customary for children to wear their new clothes to welcome in the new year. Red was the color of choice, as it was considered a lucky color to bring a bright and prosperous new year. This was the one time of the year when my mother would splurge and buy us new clothes and shoes.

The tradition was to call on relatives and close friends. The visits and greetings were done in order of seniority. In our family that meant paying respects to our grandparents first and then any elderly relatives and uncles and aunts, followed by close friends. Led by our parents on those visits, we walked through streets littered with red casings of burnt firecrackers, all while dodging more firecrackers being lit in front of businesses and institutions. My mother carried treats she had made along with fruits of bright red and orange colors symbolizing money and fortune. We followed close behind hoping to get lucky money from as many relatives and family friends as we could meet. At the end of the New Year holidays, we would be giddy with excitement as we counted our take of lucky money.

A significant festival in the spring is the Ching Ming Festival. It normally falls in early April and is similar to Memorial Day in the United States. It is the day when relatives flock to their ancestors' graves. Respect for one's heritage is an important Chinese value. Every respectable Chinese is expected to honor the ancestral dead. The indigenous Chinese families carry incense sticks and paper offerings shaped to look like money, clothing, houses, and even cars. These paper offerings are burnt at the gravesite in the belief that those who have passed will still be able to enjoy these earthly luxuries in their after-worlds. Chinese families also bring foods such as roast suckling pig, steamed chicken, fruit and wine, which are offered to the ancestors during the ceremony but are usually eaten up after the offering.

Because we were a Christian family, we didn't follow the pagan traditions. On the day of the Ching Ming Festival, we brought flowers to the graves of our ancestors who were buried in Macau's cemeteries. Many people also traveled to mainland China to visit the graves of their ancestors. I never did, or my parents never took me. In my memory, we didn't have many ties to mainland China, where our ancestors came from. What I learned about my family's past was mainly from passing comments and occasional stories.

Another festival that was one of my childhood favorites was the Mid Autumn Festival. It generally takes place in late September or early October. It is something like a fall harvest festival. The custom is to gather the family to admire the moon and eat moon cakes. These cakes are only made once a year during this festival. They are made with sweet lotus seed paste with a salted egg yolk in the center, mimicking the moon.

Our restaurant sold moon cakes for the Mid-Autumn Festival. It was an elaborate undertaking that required a lot of extra help. Weeks before the festival, my father would hire a dozen temporary workers who sat around big round tables picking out the bitter centers of lotus seeds. He also hired electricians to create the most spectacular moving lantern display over the marquee of the restaurant. This was to attract the attention of the would-be moon cake buyers, similar to how Macys and Carson Pirie Scott department stores in the United States compete for attention during the Christmas season with Christmas animation window displays.

This was one of the most exciting of all festivals. The streets were bustling with people milling around looking at the light shows over the marquees of restaurants. We children were allowed to purchase a colorful lantern of our choice and run around in the crowded streets. Street vendors of every kind also took advantage of the crowds out and about. At night, after the restaurant closed, the whole family would go up to the rooftop where tables and chairs had been set out for the autumn feasts. There we would eat our fill and watch the glorious full moon, and listen to stories of the jade rabbit who lives on the moon. It was a happy and fun occasion.

When I think of all the colorful festivals in Macau, I can't help but think about the Macau Grand Prix. Though not a Chinese festival, the Macau Grand Prix is a Macau tradition that has taken place every year in November since 1954. It started as an amateur event for local motoring enthusiasts, and today is one of the world's most exciting car races with a city circuit, called the Guia Circuit. The racing circuit runs for about four miles around Macau's winding streets and is considered one of the most challenging courses on the international motor racing scene. For two days, the narrow twisting streets of the Guia are turned into a racetrack showcasing the top champions in the world of auto racing.

During the days of the Grand Prix, the whole city palpitated with excitement: the noise of the engines, the crowds of tourists, and the colorful flags on the streets. My brothers and I never missed the Grand Prix. We couldn't afford to purchase seats at the viewing stand, but the race could be viewed from many spots around the circuit where bleachers were set up. We would sit at strategic spots close to the finish line to watch the race. As the drivers got close to the finish, we would run along the course to chase after the would-be champions. For one week in this sleepy little town, the Macau Grand Prix changed the rhythm of life for the Macau people, and brought glamour and excitement to their humdrum lives.

8

Of Tricycles and Things

WHEN I LOOK back on my life, I am amazed by how certain events in my childhood shape the deepest fears and anxieties and in turn the hopes and dreams in my adult life. How could things that happen in such a short span of my life have such a profound impact on the rest of my life?

I remember this like it was yesterday.

My brother Charlie and I wanted a tricycle. We had been begging for one for a long time. On the way to the park one day, we stopped by the store down the street to check one out. There it was—a beautiful fire engine red three-wheeled spectacle that hung from the ceiling of the store for all to see. The shiny chrome on the tricycle beckoned to us to take it home. Charlie and I wanted it bad. We carried on with the begging and whining, which went on for more than half an hour. The storeowner was impatient. My mother was flustered, but money was short. There were six mouths to feed. Buying the tricycle would take away from something else. In the end, to our disappointment, we walked out of the store empty-handed. On the way home from the park, my mother discovered that she had been pickpocketed. She had lost the money she could have used to buy us that tricycle. I heard her sob that night when she told my father what happened. She was so sorry that she hadn't bought us that tricycle.

The incident had a huge impact on me. When I looked at my mother, I realized that the hardest thing about being poor wasn't that she couldn't get what she wanted, but that she couldn't give her children what they wanted. I was so determined that this would never happen to me. When I became a mother, I worked like a demon so that I wouldn't have to deny my children the things they really wanted. I wouldn't allow myself to fail because I couldn't fail my children.

Although we didn't have a lot of store-bought stuff, we were never bored. Necessity was the mother of invention. We made our own toys and invented our own entertainment.

My friends and I made our own paper dolls. They were crude drawings on cardboard paper. For their wardrobe, we drew dresses and gowns with little tabs to attach to the doll. I had a girlfriend who was a gifted artist. Her dolls were beautiful and life-like with a well-supplied wardrobe. Lucky her. Talent was a tremendous currency when there was little real currency.

My prized possessions were my miniature plastic pots and pans that cost no more than a nickel. I would spend hours molding mud cakes and serving them to invisible guests on the dirt grounds behind our house. In school, my girlfriends and I liked to play hopscotch, jump rope, and bean-bag toss. The challenge was to make up a dozen different variations of the same games; for example, making jumping ropes out of rubber bands knotted together. My brothers were more into marbles, rocks, and fighting with sticks or make-believe weapons of any kind. They also liked anything that involved bugs and critters, like cricket fighting.

I was too squeamish to watch Charlie do gruesome things to bugs and insects, but I didn't mind spending hours together watching an ant carry a grain of rice from one venue to another. I also loved flying kites with Charlie.

We couldn't afford to buy them so we made our own. All our kites looked the same—an elongated diamond with a tail attached to the end. We made the frame by tying together two bamboo sticks in the likeness of a cross. Newspapers were used to cover the frame forming the main body of the kite. To balance the kite in flight a long strip of paper was attached to the end of the frame. My brother Charlie was the master at creating the ultimate killer kite. I watched him grind broken glass into a powder and mix the powder with a paste, which he then used to coat the strings. Instantly we had a mean kite-killing machine. Charlie was the spool handler. I was the kite runner. Across the blue skies, our homely kite sought out the best-looking store-bought kite. Then the chase was on. Once we caught up with our target, Charlie manipulated the string so that it cut into the string of the fleeing kite at precisely the right angle. The end came quickly, too quickly, I thought. Triumph was often mixed with regret. I wished that my brother would just leave those pretty kites alone.

One of our favorite places for flying kites was an open space in front of a run-down temple not far from our house. It became a playground for many kids, including us. Once in awhile, we heard about some kid having their arms and limbs blown off because some buried grenade from the last war exploded in the playground. The playground apparently was a battlefield during the war. I now come to understand what the song lyrics meant, "And there but for fortune go you or I ..."

The few luxuries we got came from visiting my uncle and his family in Hong Kong, where my parents sent us for many summer vacations. My uncle and aunt had a nice house and a maid. They were always generous to us. We went to amusement parks and restaurants. We went on rides and enjoyed carnival games. I remember tasting Wrigley's spearmint gum and Smarties candies for the first time.

But as much fun as it was, I always felt like the poor cousin from the other side of town. Hong Kong people saw Macau people as being from the backcountry. There was a huge economic disparity between Hong Kong and Macau at the time. Whereas Hong Kong was becoming a modern metropolis, Macau was still struggling to break out of rural poverty. Macau had no modern amenities such as fancy shops and restaurants. Cable television had come to Hong Kong but not Macau. Our education was considered sub-standard compared to the Hong Kong school system. The sting of being a second-class citizen simply by accident of my birthplace was a bitter pill for me to swallow.

I now know that not having *things* didn't hurt me. In fact, I now recognize that I had a happy childhood and I never wanted for anything. My formative years were filled with the joys of childhood amazements and discoveries. Yet I carry my childhood wounds with me into my adulthood. The child who badly wanted the tricycle became the adult who fears that she will not be able to provide for her family. The girl from the backcountry became the woman who desperately needs to prove that she is just as good, or better, in spite of where she came from.

I now have some clues to the question, *what drives me?*

9

Before Starbucks

WHAT LESSONS WE learn from our parents without even knowing it! Mine taught me the meaning of the saying "to pull yourself up by your bootstraps" when they found a way to begin again after they lost everything.

My parents were always struggling financially. My mother worried about money all the time. She kept a log of all of our expenses. At the end of each day, she would go through the journal and ask us if she had missed anything. Did we pay a dime or a nickel for the light bulb? How much did we spend on sewing supplies? Did we forget about the soda we shared? Where did the money go? Could we cut back on something? Would there be enough money to pay for school when the tuition comes due? The constant worry over money warped my mother's personality. Even in later years when money was no longer an issue, she couldn't change her extremely frugal habits. It pained her to spend any money unnecessarily.

We lived from day to day, borrowing from Peter to pay Paul. My father belonged to a kind of "mutual aid club" that kept his business afloat at the expense of paying sky-high interest rates. This is how it worked: A group of investors and borrowers met once a month for a dinner meeting. At the meeting, those who needed money put in a bid. The highest bidder won. This meant that whoever was most desperate for the money would pay the most interest for it. It was a short-term solution to a long-term problem. The needy just got deeper and deeper in debt. My parents were among those who were constantly struggling to pay back money they had borrowed at high interest rates. Their monetary difficulties made a big impact on me. Financial security became a paramount priority in my life and influenced many decisions I made.

I will never forget the day my parents closed down their restaurant. After struggling to keep the doors of the restaurant open for a decade, the business was no longer solvent. My parents had paid off all the creditors. All the hired help had been let go. For the first time that I could remember, our parents were just sitting around the dining table talking with us, not busy working. We counted all the money we had. It was thirty dollars and change. Five children and thirty dollars.

We went to the Catholic charities the next day and got a loaf of cheese. It was the first time I tasted cheese. Chinese people didn't eat cheese. Except for butter and powdered milk, dairy was not in our diet. My father told us, "Just imagine you are eating a whole slice of butter. That's what cheese is." We got some fresh rolls from the bakery across the street. The cheese tasted very good. No doubt, we were oblivious to our parents' anguish during this period as they struggled to figure out what they would do next to feed their family of seven.

Shortly after the restaurant closed down, my father threw himself into a business that few people had ever heard of—the coffee business. He had started this on the side a few years ago almost as an experiment. The idea was to buy raw coffee beans, then roast them, grind them, and package the coffee to sell wholesale to local eateries. The Chinese were used to drinking tea, but coffee was starting to gain popularity in the rest of the world. In Macau there was no market for coffee yet; it was the beginning of introducing coffee drinking to the Macau population. My father named his coffee distribution business *Tan Heong San* (later changed to THS), which when translated, meant *Honolulu Coffee*. I believe the idea was to give the brand an exotic feel, as coffee was still a novelty drink at the time.

From a couple of sacks of coffee beans the business slowly grew. Soon my father rented a small store to warehouse the coffee beans. The store was located next to an alley where the roasting was done. To roast the coffee, my father purchased a huge machine with a large drum that had to be rotated over a hot fire. It was the early incarnation of a roasting machine and a crude one. The fire had to be fed manually with firewood. Butter and brandy had to be added to the raw coffee beans at precise times during the roasting process to give them a deep color and rich flavor and aroma. The roasting had to be carefully monitored or the coffee would burn. Black soot from the fire and the burning peels of the coffee beans filled the air, and the winds would carry the fragrant smell down the entire street. My father's hair and clothing were covered in black soot by the end of the day. In the hot sweltering heat of the Macau summers, it was grueling work.

When I think about it, my father was a true pioneer. He was custom blending and roasting coffee long before anyone had ever heard of Starbucks. The Chinese had a long tradition of drinking tea and nothing else. What a wild idea it must have been to import coffee and roast it from scratch when the locals hadn't even developed the palate for it. Rather than selling crappy instant coffee, my father decided to be on the cutting edge of a new product. At a time when most people didn't even know what raw coffee beans looked like, he was figuring out how to import them from far-away places like Jamaica, Hawaii, Brazil, Colombia, and Ethiopia.

Many years later, when my brother Jack took over the THS business after my father retired, he became obsessed with sourcing and roasting the best quality coffee. Determined to carry on my father's legacy to offer a consistently high quality product, Jack even traveled to the United States to work with a mechanical engineering professor to design quality controls into the roasting equipment. He also worked with a packaging design company to pioneer a method of packaging that uses aerated bags to maintain the freshness of the roasted coffee. As the popularity of coffee rose with the rise of disposable income among the Macau people, Jack steadily opened a chain of THS cafés in every major Macau neighborhood, offering sandwiches, pastries, and other Chinese and Portuguese culinary delights to accompany his distinctive coffee.

Whenever I go home to Macau, one of the first things I must do is go to one of the THS cafés by my hotel or near my parents' flat. There, sitting in a bamboo chair inside the cozy Hawaiian-themed coffee outpost, sipping my cappuccino while savoring a crunchy, juicy Pork Chop Bun—an unsurpassed Macanese treat—I know I'm home.

10

Who Am I?

ONE OF MY best girlfriends was given a name that meant "It's Okay." Another female relative was named "Bring a brother." What does a name like that do to a girl's sense of self-worth?

The Chinese have never been shy about their preference for having boys and not girls. A son carries on the family name. A girl is considered a money-losing proposition. She will be married and will belong to some other family. This disdain is evident in the names given to female children. When I was young, girls were raised with low self-images and thus had low expectations of themselves and their future. Our role models were mothers and wives who were fearful, timid, and accepting of their fate.

To their credit, my parents never openly favored their sons over their daughters. In fact, I believe that my father indulged the girls more than he indulged the boys. We were the ones getting better grades in school so we got all the praise. We were the ones to whom our parents would be more likely to grant permission for special favors. My father would always give us rides on his scooter if we asked. However, if the same request came from my brothers, they would be scolded with, "Are your legs broken?"

So I grew up feeling quite conflicted about my gender. All the Chinese customs and traditions pointed to males being more important. I struggled with doubts, such as, are women inferior to men? Are our parents simply more protective of us because our future is so uncertain? Is it really possible for women to have a fulfilling future beyond marriage?

Then there is the question of my faith.

Throughout my youth, I was embroiled in a battle of two religions having been raised in a Protestant home and educated in a Catholic school.

I was raised as a Protestant by my Methodist mother. My mother had come from a deeply religious family. My grandfather was very well respected in the local Methodist church where he served as a council member. It had always been a dream of my mother's to have her family become Christians. After years of persuading my father, she finally had her way.

Sometime in my early teens, my mother took the whole family to the non-denominational church of Chi Do Tong in Macau and baptized all of us at the same time. As we grew up, our entire social life revolved around the church. We were very active in every aspect of church activities. We all took part in the choir and the youth fellowship groups. We went to Wednesday night choir practice, Saturday night youth fellowship meetings, and Sunday worship. We attended church retreats in the summer and went caroling in the streets at Christmas. When I was a high school senior, I was elected to be the president of the youth fellowship. I led prayer meetings and Bible studies. I stood up to give my testimony at candlelight sharing events. I was the model Christian youth.

When I was not busy practicing my Protestant faith at home, I was in school being brainwashed by the Catholic nuns who were my teachers. I went to early morning Mass to get extra school credit. I stayed after school to help my teachers decorate the classroom walls with drawings of cherubs and angels to earn brownie points. I learned to say Mass in Latin. I walked in Catholic processions carrying statues of Catholic saints.

Good girls in my Catholic school grew up to dedicate themselves to God by becoming nuns. Good girls from my Protestant church grew up to dedicate themselves to God by becoming missionaries.

In church, I was told that salvation would only come to Protestant Christians. At school, I was told I would go to hell if I stepped into a Protestant church. Both sides were quick to use guilt as weapons. Both exploited faith as the answer to questions that couldn't be answered. In my opaque world, I accepted my plural religions as a way of life over which I had no control. Religion was simply a part of my social and academic life. I never tried to confront the glaring contradictions.

So today I ask myself what I really believe. If everyone believes that his or her religion is the only religion that can save one's soul, then how do we know which god is the true god? If god is merciful and loving, why does he allow all the awful things to happen? What are the answers to the age-old questions, such as where did we come from and where are we going? Do heaven and hell, salvation, and everlasting life really exist? Most importantly, will I see my loved ones again when I die?

All the religious education I received in my youth failed to help me find the answers to these questions. Perhaps it is what it is. We are here to find happiness, to be the best we can be, to not hurt anyone, to live a full life, and to be kind to those who take the journey with us. Perhaps we are all praying to the same God, only that he comes in different forms. Perhaps the most important thing about being human is learning to love. Perhaps that is the only goal—to love and to be loved. If so, that is a very good goal.

My sense of citizenship is equally confusing.

I was a citizen of no country. Being born into a colony, I didn't feel allegiance to any sovereignty. I looked in the mirror and saw a Chinese face, but I didn't feel any affinity towards China. In fact, I was totally confused about which country was the real China—Communist China or Taiwan. Growing up, I was told that Communist China was evil and that the Taiwanese were the good guys who had been forced out of China. I didn't understand the politics and didn't care. In my small bubble-like world, nationalism had nothing to do with my life.

As a child of the sixties, I was born into the generation where East began to meet West in pop culture. I loved American pop music. Elvis Presley, Paul Anka, Ricky Nelson, Connie Francis, the Everly Brothers—they were my American idols. Some of my favorite songs were "Jailhouse Rock," "Diana," and "Where the Boys Are," and I would sing along while doing my homework and listening to the radio. I could sing English songs before I had really learned English. I knew all the lyrics of the pop songs by heart. I was a Chinese girl from a Portuguese colony who loved American pop culture. Talk about a conundrum.

Maybe I have some clues as to what made me the way I am. As a female, my Chinese heritage doomed me to low self-esteem, but my parents never told my sister and I that we were inferior. Our success in academics gave us the confidence that we could do anything we set our minds to. As a middle child, I didn't get any special attention, but I learned to negotiate and to adapt. I learned the people skills and street smarts I needed to survive. I was conflicted about my citizenship, my religion, and my beliefs, but my circumstances helped me to see both sides and gave me the empathy to be tolerant and open-minded. Even though my parents had few material possessions to give us, they taught us strong values and work ethics by their example. We saw their sacrifices and their struggles to keep us fed, clothed, and educated, and we knew that we were loved. Our parents also gave us the one sacred thing—our education—and the expectation that we would make something of our lives.

So this is me, full of contradictions and paradoxes. My journey took me down a long, meandering road of self-discovery. I was forever changed by the many bumps in the road. The process of survival transformed me. I found things in me that I didn't know I had. But deep down the old me lurked in the shadows, so I grew to accept the many faces of me. I'm fearful but I'm also bold. I'm shy but I'm also confident. I was raised with many biases, but I'm open to all possibilities. I'm not religious, but I believe in God and Divinity, in all their shapes and forms. I'm quintessentially American, but I'm also thoroughly Chinese. I finally see that where you come from does not define who you are; your limitations are only those that you put on yourself.

11

A Chinese Catholic Education

"THIRTY-FIVE—JACINTA Wong."

"Thirty-four—Flavia Chan."

"Thirty-three—Celina Ho."

And on and on until the last name was read.

Please God, don't let her read my name yet. Like the five finalists in the Miss America contest, I prayed that my name would be the last to be read.

Each year at the end of the school year, our standing in class would be read aloud to the entire class, starting from the bottom, with those who had earned the lowest grades, to the top, with those who had earned the highest standing in the class. It was a nerve-wracking experience. Instinctively I dropped my head to avoid catching the eyes of the teacher, lest it prompted her to call my name sooner. I stared down so hard that it felt like I was boring a hole into my desktop. To stop the uncontrollable shaking as I sat through the excruciating ordeal, I rested my chin over my tightly clasped hands. Even today, I have nightmares of waiting for my class rank to be read out in class.

The Chinese education system I grew up in was a pressure-cooker system. It had a traumatizing effect on its young people. In Hong Kong, public examination results were announced in newspapers for everyone to see. Right after the newspaper announcements, news of students committing suicide inevitably followed. It was the sad consequence of a society that valued academic success above all things.

In the Asian culture, your fate is decided very early in life. That is because the system has a way of branding the individual at an early age. If you are at the bottom of the class in the first grade, there is a strong chance that you will stay at the bottom for the rest of your life. Children who earn low rankings early on in grade school are expected to be under-achievers in life. There will be very few chances for redemption. Those at the bottom resign themselves to always be at the bottom. It is a form of self-fulfilling prophecy. So the pressure is on the moment a child enters the education system.

I was driven from a very young age to do well in school. The message was subliminal. My mother told us that she had only one expectation for us—that we would do well in school. My father's favorite sermon was "Endure the hardship for a few years (school years) and you will relax for the rest of your life." Praises were heaped on my sister Amy whenever she got the highest grades in her class. Anyone of us who didn't receive a good score would be verbally humiliated at the dinner table. The pressure was always there.

We also felt that we owed it to our parents to do well in school. In the Chinese culture, children owe everything to their parents. This was even more so in my family. My parents made uncommon sacrifices to give us an education. We didn't take that for granted.

My uncle had six children. The oldest three girls were very close to our age. They only finished sixth grade and had to go to work in garment factories making T-shirts and blue jeans. They were excellent students who had the same potential we had. To this day, they are very bitter. Their parents never made the sacrifices to send them to school because they were girls. When they compare their lives to all that my sister and I have accomplished, they are forever resentful for a life they could have had but were denied.

Getting a good education in the 1950s and 1960s was not a trivial accomplishment. Going to a private Catholic school in Macau was an exclusive privilege, generally reserved for the well-to-do if not the rich. The money parents had to pay for tuition, uniforms, books, and supplies was equal to a laborer's monthly wage. Furthermore, children who went to school couldn't help with the family business. Many children in Macau worked alongside their mothers at home doing such jobs as assembling plastic flowers. As they got older, they were sent to work in factories. So sending your child to school was a double whammy: the additional expense of tuition and books on top of the loss of income the child could have brought into the family business.

At Sacred Heart College, my sister and I were taught by nuns from Italy. They wore long grey habits that covered their bodies from head to toe, revealing only their cherubic faces. We addressed them as Mother So-and-so. Macau in the 1950s was not a top pick for the Mother Church, so most of the nuns sent to us lacked credentials. Some of them were senile, eccentric, and had other mental or emotional issues. I was unfortunate enough to have some of the worst of the bunch. Many of my teachers were neither nurturing nor academically qualified. They knew no Chinese and sometimes very little English. Mainly we learned by reading the textbooks.

The nuns were strict disciplinarians. The sound of the crackling of the cane on our desks could be heard as they walked up and down the aisles of the classroom. The misbehaving child would draw the attention of the cane to her fingers or be sent to stand in the corner of the room. In the worst cases, the nuns would put a sign on the offending child and parade her from classroom to classroom. This was the 1950s, and humiliation as a form of punishment didn't raise any eyebrows.

Our school had limited resources. Our library was the size of a small classroom. I took Chemistry without a laboratory. For gym classes, we played outside.

We were taught the Chinese way, by rote repetition and relentless drilling. Memorization was *the* method of learning. I even had to memorize the Four Gospels once. Academic success was measured by how much you could cram into your head and how much you could regurgitate. Another basic tenet of Chinese learning was accepting everything we read in the books as the final authority on the subject. We were not encouraged to think differently. The printed word was absolute. It was not to be questioned. A good student simply accepted everything she was taught. In

Chemistry, I didn't get to play with test tubes and beakers. I just had to accept the teacher's word that sulfuric acid smells like a rotten egg.

One method of memorization that turned out to be quite effective was to read our books aloud. The shouting reinforced our memory because we could hear what we were reading. We used this method in the classroom and when we were studying at home. We lived on a noisy street, so the shouting also helped us to block out the many distractions around us. We all had our favorite places in the house to do our shouting. I liked to stake out the bathroom because it had a door that could be closed—that is, until someone had to use the bathroom.

We were even taught discipline by repetition. For being late to school, we had to write five hundred times, "I will not be late again." Believe me; this form of punishment didn't change our behavior. We found different ways to speed up the writing.

We had a very heavy academic load. Many subjects were taught in both Chinese and English. We had Chinese Literature and English Literature, Chinese History and World (Western) History, reading and writing in both Chinese and English. Our Math was quite advanced; Algebra and Trigonometry were part of the high school curriculum. Conversely, we had very little time to spend on sports, music, and the arts. I passed my Physical Education classes just by standing in the corner chatting with my friends.

In Biology, we skipped the entire chapter on human reproduction. My prudish nunnery teachers decided that we didn't need to know anything about our reproductive organs. She dragged her feet the entire semester, avoiding that chapter until we ran out of time. Thanks to my Catholic education, I was shockingly ignorant on the subject of sex when I left for the United States at the age of nineteen. I had never learned anything about sex and how babies were made.

My mother did little to enlighten me on the subject. When I first got my period, I thought I was bleeding to death. My mother never explained anything. The grim look on her face told me what I needed to know. Becoming a woman was a bad thing. I was doomed.

Add Catholic teachings to a strict Chinese upbringing and you have a child who was brainwashed and confused about her morality, her sexuality, her beliefs, and her values. My education was geared not so much to prepare me for life as to prepare me for work. I had distorted ideas about what was important in life. Those who were good in math and sciences were touted as the smart ones. Excelling in music, art, and sports meant that you were a good-for-nothing.

The fifth year in our six-year high school system was set aside for vocational training, such as typing and shorthand. Most girls in my school aspired to be secretaries and receptionists. They had visions of themselves sitting by the window outside the office of some executive, a male executive of course, looking pretty and doing a little typing in between running to pour him more coffee. Not me. I had no idea how I would go to college, but I couldn't see myself as a secretary, clerk, or receptionist. I was determined that I had no use for such training. I would skip Form 5 and go directly to Form 6.

To skip Form 5, I had to prove that I was academically capable of going to college. Only the top three students in the class were allowed to skip Form 5. Unfortunately for me, I ranked No. 4 in my class. But I wasn't going to give up. With the help of Amy, who had easily skipped one grade, we went to the principal's office and pleaded my case. I couldn't remember how, but amazingly we convinced her. I skipped vocational training. The victory had little to do with spending another year in high school and everything to do with proving to myself that I was destined for college. Was it a real victory? In hindsight, I realize that I was more egotistical than smart. My ego had driven me to take a risk that could have ruined my hope for a decent job, and I had no backup plan.

I read Shakespeare, Hemingway, Jane Austen, Charles Dickens, and many old classics. My mother told people that I liked to read. The truth is I liked to write more than I liked to read. I loved the power of the written word, how words could stir emotions, enhance understanding, and change the way you see things. I felt that power at my fingertips when I wrote.

José da Costa Nunes, the Bishop of Macau, came to visit Macau in November 1965. The Second Vatican Council of the Catholic Church (Vatican II) opened in October 1962. Pope John XXIII wanted the Council to inject new life and energy into the Catholic faith to better serve the needs of their fellow Christians.

Cardinal Nunes had attended Vatican II. In honor of his first-time visit to Macau, a writing competition on the theme of Vatican II was held for the local Catholic high schools. Every grade from Form 4 to Form 6 would send three students to the competition. Since there were three Catholic girls' high schools in Macau, a total of twenty-seven girls were picked from the best writers of their schools. It was the first of such competitions. Cash prizes in the amounts of $100, $200, and $300 were to be awarded to the top three winners.

I was one of the three girls picked from my grade in my school. We were not told the subject of the writing competition, but we knew it had to do with what came out of Vatican II. The teachers could offer little help. Most of them were not versed in the affairs of the Catholic Church. After all, Macau was only superficially Catholic. The Church's influence on the Chinese people in Macau had more to do with its schools and charities than the Catholic faith.

I didn't have high hopes for winning the competition. I was not Catholic, so I was surprised to even be picked. But I wanted to win. I decided that to do so, I must have a plan. Since we were not told about the topic, there was little we could do to prepare for the contest. I knew, however, that I needed something to give me an edge.

My secret weapon: a quote from the Pope.

I memorized a quote out of an English newspaper taken from Pope John XXIII's opening address in September 1963. The address stressed the four principles he had set out for the council: defining the nature of the church, restoring unity among Christians, renewing the church, and starting a dialog with the modern world. My plan: No matter the subject of the essay, I would use this quote.

In the spring of 1965, I entered the room for the writing competition with twenty-six other young writers. We were given two hours to write about "The Role of the Laity in the Catholic Church."

One of the most significant ideas that came out of Vatican II was that there ought to be greater participation by lay people in the liturgy. This led to permissions being granted in the mid-1960s to celebrate most of the Mass in vernacular languages, which was by far the most impactful change on the lives of everyday Catholics in the history of the Church.

One month later, the results of the competition were announced at the morning assembly in the playground. Our school had won second place. I was the winner. My prize money was $200. I had won the first Catholic Girls High School Essay competition and I was not even Catholic!

My parents didn't make a big deal of my win. They basically chalked it up to a small academic achievement. After all, it wasn't as if I had won a Math test or first honors in my class. It was very much a non-event to them.

But for me, what I won that day was not just the prize money. I won personal validation. For the first time in my life, I felt special. I felt that I might have special gifts.

When I graduated from high school, there was no prom, and graduation itself was not an event to be celebrated. It meant the end of the road. What do you do now? Nobody from Macau in 1967 expected to go to university unless they were from a rich family and could afford to go overseas to America, the United Kingdom, Canada, or Australia. There were two universities in Hong Kong at the time, but no student from Macau had ever made it into a Hong Kong university. That's because the path to Hong Kong universities was through the Hong Kong school system, a system that automatically disqualified Macau students.

There were no jobs in Macau when I graduated from high school. Factories had come to Macau. The gambling industry also got started around this time. For a young girl with a high school education who didn't want to go to work in a factory or a casino, there were few other prospects.

12

Leaving Home at Seventeen

WHEN I GRADUATED in the summer of 1967, I was anxious and worried. What would I do now? I needed to find a job, and I needed to do so quickly. If I didn't get a job during that first summer, chances were that I would be stuck in Macau forever. In a Hong Kong newspaper I found an ad for a fourth-grade English teacher in an all-girls school named True Light Middle School (TLMS). I got a seven-day visitor's visa to go to Hong Kong for the interview.

The principal of TLMS, Dr. Ho Chong Chong, had a reputation as a pioneer of girls' education and as a strict disciplinarian. TLMS was a boarding school known for its strict code of behavior and its emphasis on academics. The girls who went to TLMS were taught to be modest, obedient, and studious—all virtues for a good girl in the Chinese culture. The attire for the school told the story. Everyone in the school, including the teachers, wore the same shapeless pale blue Chinese gown that draped loosely over the entire body to fall a couple of inches below the knees. The sack-like dress was designed to cover up every hint of youthful femininity. All the girls wore their hair straight and short, cut even with the ears. No makeup, jewelry, or any kind of ornamentation was allowed. From a distance, everyone in the school looked alike. In fact, that was the whole idea. Individuality was discouraged. Conformity was the goal. This was 1967, and the TLMS education reflected the moral standard of the time.

I was a seventeen-year-old graduate of a relatively liberal school with foreign influence. The thought of being trapped inside a strict convent-like all-girls school was terrifying. But I needed a job and this was the best job I could get. It would be a respectable job, and more importantly, it would allow me to move to Hong Kong to seek future opportunities. It was to be my first job interview, and I took it very seriously. With no prior interviewing experience, I sat down and made a plan.

In case you're wondering how a seventeen-year-old high school graduate could get a teaching job in Hong Kong, the answer is simple. It was a matter of supply and demand. This was during a post-war period, and many school-age children had been born. There were only a handful of university-graduated students from the two Hong Kong universities. Most did not aspire to be low-paid schoolteachers. There were no regulations governing the qualification of teachers. Recycling high school graduates into grade school and high school teachers was the obvious solution.

Dr. Ho was a progressive feminist educator. She knew that her girls needed to learn English. The fact that I came from Macau actually gave me an advantage over candidates from Hong Kong. To her it meant that I was a simple, unaffected girl, and as such, I would fit well with the school's ideals of modesty and humility. I also knew that I needed to impress her with my English ability. So that was my plan—I would greet her in English and answer her questions in English.

Word by word, I wrote down my interview dialog.

"I am very pleased to meet you, Dr. Ho."

"I love teaching. I was a tutor in high school."

"Yes, Macau is a great place to grow up. We live a simple life. We don't have a lot of toys or entertainment. We love books."

I wrote the script to cater to my interviewer. Every sentence was carefully crafted and rehearsed. Every question was anticipated and the response planned. Even though I was by no means fluent in speaking English, I knew Dr. Ho hardly spoke any herself. All I had to do was to impress her and lead her to my planned questions.

The plan worked. She called me the day after my interview and told me I was hired. I couldn't believe it. I had beaten the odds—a girl from

Macau getting a teaching job in Hong Kong with a highly respected school! It was the first of many confidence-building experiences in my life.

I soon found out that I was not prepared to be a teacher. I lacked the maturity, the compassion, and the patience to be a good teacher. Furthermore, I had never received any formal teacher's training. My two years as a grade school teacher were nothing less than torturous. I hated every minute of it. The children were well behaved and adoring. They were everything a teacher could ask for. But I was ill prepared to teach, emotionally and academically. I knew from the first day that I couldn't do this for a living. Teaching would not be a long-term career for me.

Let me pause here to say that my attitude towards my job had nothing to do with how I feel about the teaching profession. My daughter is a high school teacher and I am so proud of her. I truly believe that teaching is more than a job; it is a calling. You have to have the passion and the right motivation for teaching or it will not be a satisfying experience.

To take the job in Hong Kong, the first thing I needed was a place to live. I had met an older teacher who lived a short distance from the school. She was a widow, and she was trying to supplement her income by renting out rooms to teachers who needed housing. I couldn't afford one of her regular bedrooms, so I rented the maid's room in the back of the kitchen of her flat. The room measured approximately seven feet by six feet, not very much bigger than a closet, but it did have a window and there was a toilet next door.

My father brought me to Hong Kong and took me shopping for some basic necessities for my first "apartment." The room came with a bunk bed. I slept on the bottom bunk and used the top bunk for storage. The only other piece of furniture that fit in the room was a small desk with a hutch. The desk was my dining table, my writing table, and my dressing table all in one. It is amazing how little one can live with.

When life is harsh and bleak, we find comfort in the smallest things. The ordinary things that somehow brighten up our dreary lives become lifelong treasures. Among the things my father bought me was a new comforter, a buttery yellow satin comforter that I loved. During those chilly winters when I was living alone in Hong Kong, my comforter became my security blanket. I loved cuddling up to its cool surface and feeling the softness of the satin fabric against my skin. Years later when I went to America, my yellow comforter was one of the few things that I took with me. My children also fell in love with my comforter. My daughter had it as a baby blanket until she was six years old. She couldn't part with it even after it became so torn and tattered that I had to secretly throw it away.

It was in those first months in Hong Kong that I found out what it was like to be alone. For the first time in my life, I had to cope with everything all by myself. From cooking to laundry, I had to learn to do things that I had never done before. My mother had spoiled us at home, and we never lifted a finger to do any housework. She had told us that our only job was to study hard and do well in school. Everything else was done for us. So I had no life skills. I hardly knew how to boil an egg or sew on a button. Washing and ironing were real chores to me. I didn't know how to clean. I hated these household chores and I was miserable with the way I had to live. I no longer came home to a noisy house full of people I loved. The loneliness was overwhelming. I was so homesick that I cried all the time.

For the next two years, I would spend almost every penny I earned going home to Macau every chance I got. That meant going on the ferry-boat that went between Hong Kong and Macau every weekend. The boat ride took four hours, but the boarding and disembarking added another three to the trip. I would board the boat Saturday afternoon as soon as I got off from work and come back on the overnight ride on Sunday so that I could make it to work on Monday morning. Most days I didn't get enough sleep. In fact, I was so tired that I would catch a quick shut-eye while standing with my back to my students during a reading or writing class. The constant fatigue made my life even more miserable.

For the first time in my life, I learned about things that I had never known or even heard about. One was the taboo subject of homosexuality.

This is the story of Sue.

While I was still living at home in Macau, I had a circle of friends from church, very nice girls who sang in the choir, joined the youth fellowship, and went to church every Sunday. We all went to the same high school except for Sue. Sue was a friend of a friend.

I had always noticed that Sue was different. She regularly wore pants and her hair was cut short like a boy's. She walked with a boyish gait. She talked with a boldness that made me blush. Not very ladylike, I thought. I didn't know anything about sex. I had no idea that some people were homosexuals, or even what that meant. There were whispers that Sue liked this girl we will call Sam, who was also from our church. She was a very pretty girl with long chestnut hair, gorgeous brown eyes, and an exotic Eurasian face. Sam was very popular and every girl's envy. Besides being beautiful, she had a great voice and often sang solo in the choir. Everyone loved Sam. So imagine my shock when I caught Sue and Sam kissing in a back room one night. I couldn't believe what I saw. I refused to believe what I saw.

I didn't see Sue for a few years until I went to work in Hong Kong. She was a close friend of my friend Mandy. One Saturday evening, Sue invited us to go out for a drink and a movie with her. We went to a bar and we all had orange juice. Sue was in a funny mood that evening. She was making a lot of jokes that went over my head. When we left the bar and walked outside, there was a chill in the evening air, and I couldn't stop shivering. Sue took off her jacket and put it on me. I thought that was such a chauvinistic act to come from a girl, but I liked it.

We passed by a drugstore and Sue made a bet with us that she could get prescription sleeping pills without a prescription. Minutes later, she came out of the store with a bottle of what was supposed to be sleeping pills. We were too naïve to know anything about prescription drugs so we were not so impressed.

Then we passed by a record store. The song "Kiss Me Goodbye" was the hit song at the time. Sue surprised us by going into the store and buying each of us the hit single. Very generous of her, I thought.

Afterwards we went to the movies. The movie we saw was a sad, depressing drama called *Interlude*. It was about an illicit affair that had to end. In the middle of the movie, Sue reached over and touched my hand. Her hand was so cold it sent chills through my body. The feel of her hand touching mine gave me a really odd feeling, but I had no idea why.

After the movie, we said goodbye to each other and took separate transportation to go home. I asked Sue how she was getting home. She told me that she was going to take Bus #18. I found it odd because there was no Bus #18. I thought she was joking, just as she had been doing all evening, even commenting one time that ten years from now her bones would be fit for beating drums (a Chinese saying referring to those who had long since passed away).

The following week I was at work when I got a phone call from my friend Mandy. She was hysterical. Sue had been found dead from an overdose of sleeping pills. She had returned home from a cooking class, cooked a chicken for her parents, said goodnight, and went to bed as if nothing was out of the ordinary. She had told her parents that she would be going abroad to study and that she had purchased a plane ticket and would be leaving at the end of summer. She left a bit earlier, much earlier than any of us could ever imagine.

It took some time for me to realize that when she had mentioned Bus #18, she was referring to the Chinese context of eighteen layers of hell. Her bones are indeed fit for beating drums by now, as it has been over forty years since Sue killed herself.

A few days after she died, we gathered in Mandy's house to open a package that Sue had sent to all of us by registered mail the day before she took her life. Inside was a letter that would break my heart. In the letter, Sue explained that this was something she had to do. She asked us not to be sorry for her. The only regret that she had was that she had not been born a boy.

We later found out that Sam had left her for a guy. Nobody at the time could possibly understand Sue's heartache and desperation. Homosexuals were not accepted in our society in the 1960s. Life held no hope, no promise for one as different as Sue. She could see no way out.

I didn't believe in ghosts and spirits, but I couldn't explain what happened that day at Sue's funeral. As her coffin was being lowered to the ground, I heard somebody whistling the tune of "Kiss Me Goodbye." I looked at Mandy. She was white as a ghost. She had heard it too.

I could relate to Sue because I too was an outsider. My favorite song was Janis Ian's "At Seventeen." The wistful lyrics told of young girls with such low self-esteem that they saw themselves as ugly ducklings who would never know the joy of receiving valentines, who were never picked for anything (including when choosing sides at basketball), who indulged themselves in fantasies of make-believe lovers, and who dreamed about living the lives of more popular girls. It was a song about me, at seventeen.

In the summer of 1967, I was coming into my womanhood when I moved to Hong Kong. For the first time, I realized that I wanted the attention of the opposite sex. But when I looked into the mirror, I saw a homely young woman who had no sense of herself. I had no idea what clothes would look good. I didn't know what hairstyle would flatter my face. I wore conservative clothes with muted colors to be indistinguishable in a crowd. I carried myself in a timid, awkward way that betrayed my total lack of self-confidence. At seventeen, my low self-esteem was palpable.

On the occasions when I felt overwhelmed by sadness, I would climb up to the rooftop of the building and yell out "I love you" to the skies. What wacky bizarre behavior for a seventeen-year-old! I had no idea to whom I was talking. Maybe it was to some make-believe lover. Maybe it was to myself. Sadly, I now recognize the manic-depressive symptoms of a young woman who was desperate to be noticed and to be loved.

Part Two

The Run-Away Horse:
In Search of my American Dream

13

Coming to America—The Mountain of Gold

I DON'T BELIEVE in luck but I do believe in fate. Luck is leaving things to chance; fate, or a better word—destiny, is taking action to define your path. I met my destiny in a chance meeting and an overheard conversation. It changed my life forever.

My sister Amy was the first to leave home. She had met a nice young man named Fred who was to become her husband. Together they went to London where Amy started her studies in law.

"You can come over to England by applying to be a nurse." She told me. "Nurses get a stipend and you will be able to support yourself."

The prospect of being a nurse didn't excite me. I had a very high propensity for empathy and a very low threshold for pain. Being a nurse would be pure misery. I couldn't imagine sticking needles into patients or cleaning up bodily liquids and other unimaginable messes. I would be too squeamish to cope with blood and gore. No, nursing was not for me.

But that was not the only reason why I didn't want to go to England. I didn't want to follow in the footsteps of my sister. All my life I was told how clever and beautiful she was. I was the invisible sister. If I went to England, I would never step out of Amy's shadow. I needed to forge my own path. I needed to make my own mark. It didn't matter what it would take.

One day my brother Charlie came home with a friend. It was a casual acquaintance and an uneventful meeting. But as they were chatting away in the living room, my ears perked up. His friend was talking about an agency in New York that was helping foreign students go to the United States to study. The agency was called the *Catholic Information Center*, a very nondescript name.

Is this for real? Would some organization that knows nothing about me be willing to help me? I had watched a couple of my classmates leave Macau to go overseas to study. Their families had the means to send them. I was filled with envy when Amy sailed off to the U.K. with her fiancé to attend law school. Amy had always been the lucky one. But I didn't dare to want that for myself. With no money and no connections, the prospect of this happening to me was nil. But hearing the discussion made my heart pound. A glimmer of hope lit up within me. I asked Charlie's friend for the address of this organization. I had never done anything like this before, but I sat down and wrote an introductory letter asking for help to go to the U.S. to pursue an education.

To my surprise, they actually wrote back. I was told to take the TOEFL (Test of English as a Foreign Language) and to submit an essay, written in English and in Chinese, explaining why I wanted to go abroad to study and what I would do with my education. At eighteen, the only real life experience I had was my job as a fourth grade teacher. So that was what I wrote.

"I want to go to America to get a degree in Education so that I can come back and help children in Hong Kong."

It was not a lie, but it was not the truth either. I hated my job as a teacher, but I really didn't know what I wanted to do with my life. Helping to better young minds sounded like the right thing to say. I had no idea what was my calling, and I hadn't lived enough yet to find my passion. I only wanted to get out of my dead-end life. I wanted something better. I wanted to go anywhere that would offer me the hope of a future. I didn't care where.

Months went by and I didn't hear back. Then in the spring of 1969, I got a letter of acceptance from a school called Barat College, in a town called Lake Forest, in the state of Illinois. Lake Forest is about thirty miles from a big city I had heard something about—Chicago.

I was so excited when I got the letter from Barat College that I took the first ferry home that weekend to tell my parents about it. This was it— my ticket to an education. I had heard about America, but very few people I knew left home to go to America. Most of my schoolmates went to Canada, Australia, or the United Kingdom where they had relatives. America seemed like such an exciting, new country even though I had no friends or family there.

My parents didn't share my excitement.

"What is America like? Who will take care of you there? What if you get sick? How will you support yourself? Will there be bad people who will take advantage of you? Who will we call if something happens to you?"

The questions kept coming. My parents had no money to give me, no- body to contact to find out how I was doing. They had no idea of the life I would have in America. They would not be able to send me a ticket to come home if things didn't work out.

My mother was adamant that I should not go. I pleaded with my fa- ther. In the end, he came through for me.

"Let her go," he said to my mother. "This is her chance to get an edu- cation. She doesn't want to be stuck in Hong Kong in a job she doesn't love for the rest of her life. This is what she wants. Let her find her way."

I realize now what a gift it was for my father to let me go. He was giving me the chance to become who I am and to have the life that I enjoy today. But my parents didn't know it then. They didn't know anything about the country I was going to. They didn't know how I would come back or if I would ever be back. It was a heart-breaking choice; It's like vol- untarily giving your child away so that she might have a chance for a better life.

For the next six months, I prepared for my trip abroad. Chicago was a very cold city, I was told. I bought a winter coat. I took my lung x-rays, a requirement for entering the country. I tried to save as much money as I could. I was making $500 H.K. a month, a sum equivalent to $62 U.S. It was barely enough money to pay for my monthly expenses of rent, food, and transportation, so putting money away for my upcoming trip was a hardship. I also needed to buy an airline ticket. It was going to be my first trip on an airplane.

Behind the excitement, however, there was also fear and sadness. I would be leaving home for good. Who knows when I would be back again? Was this going to be the big adventure I had hoped for, or would there be danger and disaster waiting for me?

On August 28, 1969, I said goodbye to my family and boarded a chartered flight on Transcontinental Airlines headed for America. My airfare was $280 U.S. I flew to the States with my childhood friend Magdalen. She was going to be staying with a relative in Boston. I was going to Illinois where I didn't know a soul.

My port of entry to America was San Francisco International Airport. There I said goodbye to Magdalen. Her relatives were picking her up for a brief vacation in Los Angeles before she would go on to Boston. I would not see her again for another five years. As I walked from the international terminal to the domestic terminal, I was shivering and petrified. It was late summer but the early morning air was chilly. In the orange glow of the California morning, I must have looked like a pathetic figure—a young girl in an ill-fitting houndstooth suit holding a steel suitcase in one hand, and carrying a tubular carton containing my lung x-rays in my other hand. I felt all alone. With not a soul to call on, no money to take the next plane home, no means to communicate with my family, Macau might as well have been a million miles away. For the first time in my life, I was truly on my own. The gravity of that reality hit hard as I boarded my flight to Chicago, my final destination.

When I got off the plane, I literally had no place to go. The gate attendant took me to the Traveler's Aid office. I had a phone number from my sister's friend who was supposed to give me a ride to the campus of Barat College, the school I was going to attend. When they tried calling that number, however, it was a disconnected number. In desperation, the Traveler's Aid office called the school, but the campus was not supposed to open until after Labor Day in September. Luckily, they found a student who volunteered to pick me up.

I have unfortunately since forgotten her name. I will call her Kathleen here. She was a senior with one semester left. An Education major, she had come to the campus early to prepare for her student teaching in the fall semester. It was my first encounter with an American girl. Kathleen brought me to the campus of Barat College on a warm summer afternoon. It was a beautiful campus with stately red brick buildings and luscious grounds. The campus was situated in the affluent neighborhood of Lake Forest, a neighborhood of old money and extraordinary wealth. My first impression of America was that the whole country would be like Lake Forest. No wonder the Chinese nickname for America was "Gold Mountain," which literally meant streets paved with gold. Lake Forest fit that description.

Barat College was located thirty miles north of Chicago, Illinois. The college was named after Saint Madeleine Sophie Barat, a Sister of the Sacred Heart Order of Nuns. It was a tiny all-girls liberal arts college with just over three hundred students. Barat was well known for its Fine Arts program. It also had a reputation as a finishing school for young socialites. For a nineteen-year-old from the third-worldish backcountry of Macau, this couldn't have been a more foreign landing.

The centerpiece of this Catholic college campus was a stunning Georgian Revival structure called The Old Main that housed administrative offices, classrooms, music and art studios, a bookstore, a cafeteria, the Sacred Heart Chapel, and a performing arts theater. It was to become the center of my world for the next three and a half years.

My memory of what happened the day I arrived at Barat College is surprisingly foggy, even though everything I saw, smelled, and heard must have been so stunningly alien to me. I was suffering from serious jet lag after flying more than twenty-five hours, plus a layover in San Francisco. On top of that, my body clock was turned upside down, as Chicago time was thirteen hours behind Hong Kong time. I arrived at Barat bewildered and feeling a thousand emotions. Swelling through my body was utter fatigue.

My residence hall was Dougherty Hall, a spanking new mid-rise building with a handsome façade and a grand piano in the reception area. An elevator brought me to my room, a light-filled, spacious room with tall closets, a beautiful huge desk, and a bed with a thick cushy mattress. I had a "we are not in Kansas anymore" moment, but I was more overwhelmed than impressed.

After Kathleen left and the door was finally closed, I was overcome with emotions. There I was, all alone. No matter how things turned out for me, I would not be able to go home. Whatever lay in my future, I would have to deal with it, all by myself. There would be no one to help me. I cried as if my heart had broken into a thousand pieces. I sobbed so loud that the whole dorm would have heard me had there been anyone there. Eventually I felt asleep. In my sleep, I couldn't stop crying.

I remember waking up and seeing that it was twilight outside. It would have been morning at home. My body was still on Hong Kong time. I must have slept over twenty hours. I needed to find the bathroom. When I opened the door, I found a pile of stuff on the floor. There was an orange plush dog with a green scarf, an assortment of magazines, and a stack of hangers. On top of the pile was a note from Kathleen. She wanted me to have something to read and she thought I could use the hangers. The orange Snoopy was her gift to cheer me up.

I wish I had kept that note, but I did keep Snoopy for more than a decade. I never saw Kathleen again, but I will never forget what she did for me on that first day of my arrival in America. I wish that I could meet Kathleen again and thank her, really thank her, to let her know how much her act of kindness meant to me.

Do you know what it was like for a nineteen-year-old to be dropped off in a totally foreign country in 1969? Communication was very different then. There was no e-mail, no Internet, and no cell phones. A long-distance call from Illinois to Macau cost twenty-seven dollars for the first three minutes. Postal mail took one week to get to Macau and another to come back. The sense of isolation was mind-numbing. The homesickness I felt as a young woman thousands of miles away from home was all-consuming. I missed my mother. I missed my family. I missed the smell and taste of Chinese cooking. I missed the chattering of Cantonese voices. I missed the familiar streets and buildings. I even missed the smell of diesel and the noisy jostling crowds that had been such a part of my life in Hong Kong.

A simple twist of fate had landed me in America. With less than a hundred dollars in my pocket, knowing no one, and speaking little English, what would happen from here on was all up to me.

14

In the Land of Oz

I LOVE AMERICAN children's stories. One of my favorites is *The Wonderful Wizard of Oz*. I like to think of Dorothy's companions on her way to the Emerald City as portraits of myself, except I was the Scarecrow, the Tin Woodsman, and the Cowardly Lion all in one. Like them, I lacked the confidence to see my potential. Like them, I had always had the brains, the heart, and the courage to handle whatever life dealt me, but it took a series of life-changing encounters along the yellow brick road to discover what I had inside of me.

Like Dorothy looking for her Emerald City, I had no idea what America was like. My faint concept of America was based on the few movies I had seen. They really didn't prepare me for the America I was about to face.

English was spoken in a strange way. *Biscuits* here go by the name of *cookies*. Instead of standing in a *queue*, you *line up*. You don't *post* a letter; you *mail* it. I soon learned that *neat* didn't mean *tidy*, and that it was good to be *cool*.

And the food—how utterly strange was the food! Anyone who knows me knows that I am a food fanatic. I love to eat. This is a girl who came to the States with her own brand-new place setting of flatware: a fork, a knife and a spoon that I had bought from a large department store in Hong Kong. In spite of that, I had a very difficult time with American food.

Nothing in American cuisine resembled what I thought food was supposed to be. Nothing.

Let's take the salad. All my life I thought vegetables were supposed to be cooked. Not in America. Everything and anything could be eaten raw, just like how bunnies and cows would eat it. The only difference was this sweet, tangy, gooey, runny liquid called salad dressing that was piled on top to cover up the unpalatable taste of raw vegetation.

In a Chinese dinner, we ate lots of vegetables topped with small amounts of meat. This formula was reversed in America. Large portions of beef, chicken, or pork were piled onto the dish with a tiny decoration of vegetables. In fact, vegetables had such an unimportant role in a meal that hardly any thought went into cooking them, so they were simply boiled until they were pale and tasteless. A Chinese meal wouldn't be a meal without rice. Here rice made a rare appearance, but you could always count on large helpings of potatoes, spaghetti, and bread. Worst of all, there was no fresh fish, none whatsoever. This was the early 1970s, and the only thing that American children knew about fish was frozen Gorton's fish sticks. The only other kind of fish they knew came in a can with a mermaid on it.

During my first six months in the United States, I was ill most of the time. Unable to get accustomed to the food and suffering from chronic homesickness, I often ended up in the infirmary. I had lost a lot of weight and was suffering from stress and exhaustion. Besides the demands of school, I worked multiple jobs. I needed to pay bills and tuition, and I was obsessed with building some kind of financial security for myself.

I recall a kind nurse asking if she could cook me something that would give me comfort and remind me of home. Immediately the thought of a steamy bowl of fish congee swelled in my head. I described for her what fish congee was like: beautiful slices of fresh fish swimming in a bowl of velvety rice soup, topped with ginger and scallions. Well, she did the best she could. I was appalled and disappointed when she came back with a bowl of gooey rice topped with tuna fish right out of the can!

Lake Forest was and still is a beautiful town. There are stately, million-dollar mini-mansions, some of which overlooked Lake Michigan. The homes were gorgeous, with manicured yards and gracious architectural facades. As the name of the town suggests, there were tall trees everywhere. It was mesmerizing and enchanting—the kind of quiet, gentle living that seemed to have stepped right out of a storybook. I was struck by how beautiful America was. I thought the rest of the country was just like this.

In the downtown of Lake Forest, there was a town square and a train station. There was a Marshall Fields Department Store that to my knowledge was the only one that was privately owned. There were many lovely, one-of-a-kind stores and boutiques clustered around the town square. The ladies of Lake Forest spent their time shopping in the exquisite stores or taking the train to downtown Chicago. They could be seen in their Cadillacs waiting at the train station to meet their husbands coming home from working downtown, often with martinis in their hands.

Most of the people in Lake Forest were gracious and friendly, and many stopped to offer me rides on my way to and from downtown. I could walk everywhere. There was no concern about crimes and such. This was the early 1970s, and Lake Forest was a safe and affable landing for a foreign girl like me.

Three days after I arrived at Barat College, I walked the one and a half miles to downtown Lake Forest to look for a job. I had quickly realized that my ninety dollars was not going to last very long. My trip to Woolworth for school supplies was a wake-up call. Better find a job quick or I would be in deep trouble. I had been given a first-year scholarship of $2000, but that was not sufficient to cover tuition and room and board, which totaled more than $3000. I also needed money to buy books, school supplies, and personal necessities. Winter was approaching, and I knew the clothes that I had brought from home would not get me through the blustery cold Illinois winters. Asking for help from my parents was out of the question. They were in such dire financial straits that I would never want to burden them with my problems, especially considering that they would need to make eight dollars in Macau to send me the equivalent of one U.S. dollar.

I had asked around and found out that the biggest, fanciest restaurant in town was the Deerpath Inn. Before I came to America, many people had told me that I could make a living working as a waitress. So that was what I would do—be a waitress. Never mind that I knew nothing about the food service profession. Never mind that my spoken English was not good enough to go beyond "Hello" and "How are you?" Never mind that I had no concept of what American cuisine was all about, and no idea of what the wait staff was supposed to do. Instead, I set my sights high. I was going to work for the best establishment. If I had to be a waitress, why not start from the top?

So there it was, this beautiful restaurant/hotel called the Deerpath Inn. The architecture was reminiscent of an English country home with its ivy-covered walls and graceful, rustic interior. I mustered all my courage and walked into the main dining room. A cheerful young woman came up to greet me. In my best-rehearsed English, I asked for a job. I could see the dilemma in her eyes as she smiled at me and considered the request. In an instant, I got the urge to leave. As if I could read her mind, I sensed that my request was out of touch with reality. After all, I had no experience and I spoke almost no English. A fine establishment like this would hire only well-trained, professional wait staff.

Just as I was about to turn and run, she smiled at me with a luminous smile. Her name was Joy. How befitting! She would try me out as a break-fast server for a couple of weeks and if I did well, she would give me the job.

The following weekend, I started my career as a waitress. I soon found out that this was not just a waitress job. It was my introduction into upper crust living and fine dining in America.

The Deerpath Inn was built in 1929 by the famous Chicago architect, William C. Jones. The Inn was an English Tudor style timber and stucco two-story building modeled after the Manor House in Chiddingstone, Kent, England. The building boasted many charming architectural details including beamed ceilings and leaded windows. The dining room floors were covered in thick, rich oriental carpets. Sparkling chandeliers hung from dramatic high ceilings. In the winter, each dining room was warmed by a cozy fireplace. In the summer, the beautiful English garden could be seen from the English room, the main dining room.

The Deerpath Inn exemplified what fine living in America was all about. Rich North Shore residents came for their Sunday dinners, birthday, and anniversary celebrations. Rich parents from out-of-town came to take their college kids from Lake Forest College and Barat College out to a meal in town.

My job as a waitress at the Deerpath Inn was physically demanding. Because it was fine dining at its best, a simple serving of cereal required two layers of plates with a lace doily in between. Everything involved crisp linens, elegant place settings, and real silver tableware. The serving routine was ritualistic. Covered dishes were piled high on a huge oval serving tray. The servers had to carry the loaded tray raised up high in one hand with a folded tray-stand in the other. Ceremoniously we would walk up a steep service ramp, kick open a double door to the dining room, step up to the customer's table, set down the stand, and then carefully place the serving tray on the stand.

In time, I perfected the routine, and despite my petite five-foot frame, I managed to make the whole process look effortless. I received both praise and sympathy from my customers, who were generally impressed with how a small girl like me could handle such a physically demanding job. For that, I was rewarded with generous gratuities.

Learning about the food and drinks, however, was a very different story. I believe that you need to take a class to learn all about American cocktails. In my case, it was a crash course. I had to learn the differences between a *Rob Roy*, an *Old-fashioned*, a *Pink Squirrel*, a *Black Russian*, and a *Beefeater Martini* on the rocks with a twist. The fact that I could hardly understand the spoken English language didn't help. A Screwdriver sounded like a School Driver to me. I wrote down everything phonetically in Chinese, just so I could repeat it to the bartender and he could at least guess at what I was trying to order.

The Deerpath Inn served very elegant fare. Dishes such as Chateaubriand, Rack of Lamb and Steak Diane regularly appeared on the menu. The Dover Sole, the signature dish, was deboned at the table as the guests looked on. Caesar salad was made to order from scratch and served tableside. For dessert, flambé Cherries Jubilee and Baked Alaska were the favorites. The server had to learn how to work with the maître d' to serve each of these elegant dishes.

The menu read like the toughest textbook. Every term was something I had never heard before. Every dish was something I had never seen or tasted before. I had to learn the names of the dish, the ingredients that went into it, how it was prepared, and how it should be served.

I had to ask the right questions. Do you want your steak well done, medium, or rare? Would you like baked, mashed, or parsley potatoes? Would you like sherry in your Vichyssoise?

Mint jelly must go with lamb chops, horseradish with the prime rib, and clarified butter accompanies the lobster tail. You serve from the left and remove the dishes from the right. A steak requires very different tableware from a fish or seafood entrée.

By the time I became a proficient server, I had also acquired a very expensive taste for fine foods. Not a bad way to be introduced to a foreign culture!

Let me tell you, there were plenty of times in the beginning when I knocked over a covered dish, spilled an entrée, or crashed my whole tray of food altogether. If you had to go back to the chef to ask for a replacement dish, you were in for a harsh scolding. The maître'd would also give you a hard time if you messed up an order, if you served incorrectly, or whenever a dinner was late coming out of the kitchen. Worse yet, if you spilled something on the customer, you would most likely be fired. Luckily, that never happened to me.

But I did have my share of rude and insensitive customers. One time I asked a customer if she was done with her meal. "We in America don't like to be rushed," she told me condescendingly. Her husband was so embarrassed that he muttered something kindly to me and left me a big tip.

During the school year, I held no less than four jobs at any given time. I generally started my morning early, preparing salads in the kitchen of the school cafeteria to work off a five-hundred-dollar work-study program. After going to classes, I worked at least two evenings a week and every weekend at the Deerpath Inn. When I needed time to study, I took babysitting jobs. I also worked in the library and in the bookstore when I could get the hours.

Work became an obsession. Could I fit another babysitting job into my schedule? Could I add a couple of hours to my cafeteria job? I never said no whenever I was given an opportunity to make an extra dollar. I never turned down an evening or holiday shift because it meant earning more money. When the fall term neared its end, I began looking for jobs for the winter break. As the end of the spring term approached, I frantically searched for a summer job.

Minimum wage in 1970 was $1.60 per hour. Babysitting, however, paid only $1 per hour, and waitressing, only 95¢ plus gratuities. My jobs ran the gamut, from working as a keypunch operator for the local Lake Forest Bank, to typing transcripts for an Inventions Bureau, working as a mother's helper, house cleaning, and house painting. No job was too hard or too demeaning. They were all a means to an end. I needed to make it through college, and I was determined to do so without any debt.

On top of my hectic work schedule, I took twenty-one credit hours every semester because the tuition was the same regardless of how many credit hours I took. If I could graduate early, I would save money. It made perfect financial sense. So my life became an endless cycle of work, school, study, sleep, and more work. There was no time to do anything else. There was no time to be nineteen.

I had landed in an idyllic small town of American suburbia. My landing was no less foreign than Dorothy in the Emerald City. Culture shock didn't begin to describe what I experienced in those early days. But there was little time to acclimate. Like being dunked into the waters of a raging river, I had to quickly learn to swim or risk being drowned. My introduction to the sights, sounds, and tastes of my new country was fast and furious. There was no time for self-doubt, and even less time for self-pity. Here my wit, character, and courage would be put to the test. America turned out to be the Promised Land filled with opportunities, but my adventure had just begun. I had to maintain my focus and stay the course on the narrow and challenging yellow brick road. Like Dorothy, I had a long way to travel and many obstacles to overcome before I could find my way home again.

15

The Good, the Bad and the Ugly

LIFE AS A foreign student in an all-girls private school in the late 1960s/early 1970s was a unique experience. In a student body of three hundred white girls, there were only about twenty of us foreign students. We came from Hong Kong, Japan, Africa, and India. Our backgrounds were different but our goal was the same: We were here to seek a better future.

Why did the sisters of Barat College choose to bring over this handful of foreign students? No doubt, the Catholic Church in its compassion wanted to help those in need of a helping hand. But I also can't help but think that we were there to inject diversity into an all-white student body of mostly wealthy girls from mid-west suburbia. These girls had never met anyone with a different skin color, who spoke a different language, and dressed in an entirely different way from they did.

It was an interesting dynamic. The all-white student body was curious about us, but not curious enough to get close. They treated us somewhat like animals in the zoo, though not in a derogatory way. They were fascinated by our clothing, our food, and our language. On an economic level, they knew we were there on some kind of aid. On a social level, because we knew nothing about opera, art, and theater, we were somehow not their equals.

To be fair, we didn't try very hard to fit in. We felt self-conscious because our English wasn't good. We didn't understand the American ways.

Most of us had led a sheltered life before coming to America. We were not accustomed to interacting with foreigners and were too timid to reach out. We isolated ourselves by sticking together and staying out of the mainstream of Barat's college life. We became our own small ghetto.

For the most part, there were the African girls and the Asian girls. The African girls were a noisy gregarious bunch. They wore their colorful African garb and spent most of their time in their rooms singing, dancing, and cooking their native foods. We Chinese girls wondered why they were always enjoying themselves and having such a good time when they should be sticking to their books.

The Asian girls, by contrast, were mostly shy and quiet. We all came from very different family backgrounds. We also had very different personalities. The only thing we shared was the high expectations that our families had for us to succeed. Schoolwork was our top priority, and everyone buried themselves in books. We only socialized with each other out of the need for some sort of community and support system.

During my first year in Barat, I was joined by two other Chinese girls. It made me proud to say that of the three of us, I was the only one who made it to graduation. My roommate Ellen was a brilliant student. During our first winter break, Ellen went to New York to visit her boyfriend. She came back pregnant and soon left to join her would-be husband in New York's Chinatown. Another Chinese girl named Dana was also from Hong Kong. Dana also quit school in her second year to marry some boy who lived in Chicago's Chinatown. Three more Chinese girls from Hong Kong came to Barat during my second year. All of them eventually also got married and left to join husbands they met soon after arriving in America.

The fact that most of my fellow foreign students married early told a story of the wrenching loneliness we suffered. We were thousands of miles away from home. There was no easy way to communicate with our families. We had no one to turn to for comfort and encouragement during the struggles we faced. Few could resist the chance of not being alone anymore. My story could easily have been the same. I got married during my third year in college, but I stayed in school and finished. I will always be proud of that.

When I wrote home to my mother, I always spoke of how good everyone was to me. I didn't want her to worry. Besides there was nothing she could do. I was so far away and my parents didn't have the financial means to give me any kind of help. Why cause them unnecessary worries?

"It is your good fortune—your karma—that you always meet up with good people who are nice to you." My mother often said to me. I let her believe that.

In fact, life was not always as rosy as I painted it, and people were not as good as what I led my mother to believe. Yes, there were wonderful people, like Kathleen and Joy, who were kind to me and helped me get started in my new country. But there were plenty of other people who saw me as nothing more than an easy victim.

My first month at Barat I borrowed an electric pot from a girl who lived in the dorm room next door to make some ramen noodles. I found that it was already broken so I returned it to her. She demanded that I pay her five dollars for the cost of a new one because she insisted that I was the one who broke it. Five dollars was a lot of money to me. I never borrowed anything again.

I went to work for a family I will call the Fields who lived in the northern Chicago suburb called Northfield. They lived in an affluent neigh-borhood in a huge house. I was hired to be a mother's helper for the winter break. The Fields had four children, all under the age of seven. I cooked, cleaned, and did the laundry. I cared for the baby and took the children to the park. I worked with no days off because I had no place to go and I knew nobody. At the end of the three weeks, my "employer" sent me home without pay. She smiled and told me that since they had treated me like family, I shouldn't expect to be paid. I even had to pay for my own cab fare back to the dorm!

The experience embittered me. What kind of people would take ad-vantage of a struggling foreign student? Why would a rich family prey on a helpless young college girl? But I didn't know what I could do. There was nobody I could turn to for addressing my grievance. No doubt, she knew I was a foreigner who knew nobody and therefore an easy victim. A year later, I learned that her husband had left her for a younger woman. It made me believe in karma.

On the opposite end of the spectrum was the Wood family of Lake Forest. I had babysat one time for their nine-year-old son. He was a great kid and really didn't need me to do anything for him. That Christmas I received an invitation to come to their house as their guest. Mrs. Wood told me that they would pick me up on Christmas Eve and that I should plan to spend the night at their house. The house was a charming southern colonial style home filled with gracious furnishings and family heirlooms. When I got there, I was taken to one of the many guest rooms. The room was beautifully decorated in lavender and lace, and I felt like a princess. Later that day the Wood's grown children and their spouses began to arrive from out-of-town. They all treated me warmly as I took part in their Christmas Eve celebrations. On Christmas morning when I came down for breakfast, there was a Christmas present waiting for me. Mrs. Wood gave me a beautiful silver necklace adorned with multicolored stones. It was a Christmas I would never forget.

My mother used to say, "One brand of rice feeds a hundred different kinds of people." How could one person be so generous to a perfect stranger and another be so cruel as to take advantage of someone in desperate need? I learned that for every Field there is a Wood. It is up to us to find the good in people and not allow the few bad actors we meet to harden our hearts and turn us into cynics. Learning to forgive and to give thanks were the two early lessons I learned in my life in America. They became two of the most important lessons I would carry with me for the rest of my life.

16

Stepping Out in Barat

BARAT HAD A beautiful auditorium. It was called the Drake Theater. In its heyday, the 635-seat theater was the venue for some of the finest theatrical productions, including dance, music and plays. In the early 1970s, shows such as *Gigi*, *Alice in Wonderland*, *Stop the world, I want to get off*, and *The Fantasticks* played at the Drake to a full-house audience.

In the late spring of 1970, I put on my black leotards and blended in with the cast of a lyrical dance performance. It was the end of my first semester in Barat. It was my final—a graduating performance for my Beginners Ballet class. For good reasons I was positioned in the back. As the song "And When I Die" by the band *Blood, Sweat and Tears* boomed to an audience of dance students, I was struggling to pull my legs up high and then roll into a fetal position to the lyrics of "There'll be one child born to carry on, to carry on." It must have been hilarious, as I couldn't hold my legs up for any length of time. But the dance proved to be symbolic. My Barat days foreshadowed a new me, one that continued to change and grow.

Why did I decide to take a Ballet class when I was so downright practical and I didn't have a graceful bone in my body?

My Barat journey was nothing like what I had expected. When I came to America, I had hopes of getting a top-notch technical education. Those hopes were dashed when I landed in a small finishing school for high society Catholic girls. Barat's curriculum was filled with classes such as Art Appreciation, Art History, English Literature, Theater, Humanities, Philosophy, and Women's Studies. Over half of Barat's girls majored in Art History or Teaching. Barat didn't offer a Business major, or any technical degrees. There were no advanced math and science classes. The major that came closest to Business was Economics. I, along with five other girls in the entire student body of Barat College, majored in Economics.

Having few choices to fill my curriculum and feeling adventurous, I threw myself into subjects that were totally foreign to my Chinese upbringing. I took a class in English Literature and read *Catcher in the Rye, Dante's Inferno,* and *One Flew over the Cuckoo's Nest.* I took a class in "Zen Buddhism" and learned all about one hand clapping and reaching enlightenment. I sat through a Political Science class taught by the beloved Milton Rakove, a famous Chicago professor and author, who spoke passionately about the time when Mayor Daly's political machine ruled Chicago, a time when people only succeeded if they adhered to the unwritten rule, "Don't Make No Waves … Don't Back No Losers." I took a class in French Impressionism and ventured into the world of Claude Monet and Pierre-Auguste Renoir, where the beauty of people and landscapes were brought to life with the techniques of *light en plein air* using rapid brushstrokes and tiny dots of color. I took a class in ballet even though I knew I was a complete klutz, and I had never danced in my entire life.

If taking a class in ballet was like bungee jumping, then a semester in filmmaking was like skydiving to a timid, unadventurous girl like me. But it turned out to be one of the most memorable classes I took. My instructor was a handsome young film producer. I enjoyed listening to him talking about old classics such as the *Magnificent Seven* and the *Wild Bunch.* He loved to show footage of his favorite films, and we discussed the filmmaking techniques used as well as how to deliver impact with the camera: how different camera angles could enhance dramatic effects, the power of black and white, and music scores that stirred the soul. It was an awesome experience until I found out that for the class project, I had to write a script and make a short film!

I had grown up with no television. I had only seen a handful of movies in my life. I had never owned or operated a camera, let alone a movie camera. The professor only had two cameras available for loan, so we had to work quickly when the cameras became available. I needed to write a script, find an actor/actress, shoot the film, edit the film, and turn it in before the end of the semester. It was time to panic.

But I completed my assignment and wrote the following script for a short film that I called *Superman*:

A little boy is sitting in the family room watching TV. Flashing on the screen is the image of Superman dressed in the skin-tight blue and red costume with the "S" logo encased in a diamond design. Superman is wearing a red cape and orbiting the universe. The camera moves to the big window next to the TV. The wind is gently blowing the lace curtains open. The camera moves from the TV screen to the eyes of the little boy and then back from the little boy to the window. The little boy gets up from the floor and runs into his bedroom. He takes out his Superman pajamas and proceeds to put them on. He climbs up a stool and takes down his cape from the closet. He ties the cape over his pajamas and runs back to the family room, dragging the stool with him. From the stool, he climbs to a desk that sits in front of the window. He pushes the window open. The camera pans to the street below. The little boy's apartment is three stories up from the ground. There are cars moving in the street. It is a long way down. The camera pulls away as the little boy stands in front of the window. Then it slowly zooms in on the ground below. Without warning, the camera hurls itself to the ground giving the effect that the little boy has fallen. Then it zooms in on the little red cape on the ground three floors below and slowly zooms out. It returns to the lace curtains in the window, still fluttering gently in the wind.

It was a morbid film but I thought it delivered drama and suspense. I got a B for my project.

When I entered Barat College, I was disappointed that I couldn't pursue a degree in a field that was even remotely science or technology related. Looking back on my college years now, however, I see that my liberal arts education prepared me brilliantly for the challenges that lay ahead of me. The lessons I learned were not the ones I thought I needed to learn. They were not about practical or bookish knowledge. They were about determination, perseverance, and embracing change—lessons that not only sustained me but helped me thrive and grow throughout my life's journey.

17

Plagiarism

THINGS HAPPEN FOR a reason. Certain things happen and change you in a profound way. They may seem horrible, painful, and unfair at the time, but they eventually serve to test the limits of your character and to teach you valuable lessons. My biggest test came at the end of my first year at Barat.

In the second semester of my freshman year, I took a class in French Impressionism. I knew nothing about French art or any art for that matter. I thought this would be what is often referred to as a "basket weaving class"—one that does not require a lot of work. I had enough problems coping with the English lectures and the voluminous reading. The more academically challenging classes came with many time-consuming assignments. An art class would be a welcome change of pace and probably a cakewalk, I thought.

The class turned out to be a lot of fun. Every Saturday we took a bus to the Art Institute in downtown Chicago and looked at gorgeous paintings displayed in pristine rooms. We studied the paintings of Monet, Degas, Renoir, Cézanne, Gauguin, and all the masters of the period. We listened to our instructors' explanations of the history, the styles, and the techniques of these renowned artists. It was my first exposure to the world of art appreciation. At first, I thought I was way too practical for such nonsense, but as I explored the fascinating world of art, it opened my mind to a portal of aesthetic understanding that I didn't know existed. I found myself actually enjoying the class.

I took the course as Pass/Fail so that I didn't have to worry too much about the grade. The final exam for the course was to write a paper about one of the French Impressionistic painters we had studied. I chose to write about Claude Monet.

I had never written a term paper in my life. In my academic experience, the tests and finals had always been in the form of quizzes and questions we had to answer in the examination room. But I thought I understood the concept—to focus on a topic and put together an essay to demonstrate that I had read and understood the subject matter. I went to the library and took out every book I could find on Monet. I remember it like it was yesterday sitting at a long table in the library piled high with books and manuscripts on the artist. There I set out to cut and paste sentences and sometimes paragraphs that I liked from each book. I copied most of the words verbatim because they sounded so much better than my own. I believed that this collection of great quotes would make a wonderful paper and I should have no problem passing the course.

A few days before my first Winter Break, I went to check my mail and was surprised to find a letter in my mailbox. The letter was from the instructors (two student teachers) of my French Impressionism class. I had to read it twice before I realized what it was about. In the letter, I was told that I had failed the class because of plagiarism, a word I had never heard of before. I choked back tears and ran to my room to look it up in the dictionary.

When I read the definition of plagiarize—to take (ideas, writings, etc.) from another and pass them off as one's own—I realized I was accused of being a thief and a cheat, and *that* was why I had flunked the class!

Words could not express my shock. I couldn't comprehend what I was being charged with, but I was fully aware of the consequence. This would be a permanent red mark in my academic record. It would be a character stain that I could never erase. My hope for a bright future was dashed. What have I done? Had I come thousands of miles from home to pursue my dreams, only to be a disgrace and a failure?

For the next two days, I stayed in my room and cried my eyes out. Disappointment, shame, and despair fell on me like a heavy blanket. I had a bottle of rat poison sitting on my windowsill, and I remember staring at it for hours. Could I go on living knowing that my academic career was over? How would I tell my parents? What would happen to me now? I had come to Barat to get a college education so that I could have a chance to better my life, and now it was falling apart.

When you're forced to confront the unthinkable option of ending your life, something happens. There is no stronger instinct than the will to survive. My bleak forbidding situation woke up something deep inside of me. On the third day of moping, I regained clarity, and my thoughts came in a steady stream of consciousness, filled with feisty determination: *I must find my way out of this. I didn't do anything wrong. I will not let this destroy me.*

That afternoon, exhausted from crying, I pulled myself out of bed. I knew nothing about college governance. I had no idea of the options available to me to overturn my failed grade. Instinctively, I knew I needed to write to the person at the very top. I sat down at my desk and started writing a long letter to the Dean of the College.

In my letter, I explained that I couldn't have committed plagiarism because I had no idea what it was. I had never written a term paper and was not aware that there were rules that I needed to follow such as footnoting and naming the source. I didn't think my English was good enough so I used the words of the authors. I argued that in fact it was the same amount of work for me to "plagiarize" as it was for me to paraphrase. What could I possibly gain by plagiarizing when the course was a simple pass or fail? I had obviously done what was required: reading all about Monet and summarizing his life and his work. What I did was ignorance and not fraud. This was my first term paper in my first year as a foreign student. I asked the Dean for leniency and a second chance. I asked to be allowed to do the paper over and to earn a fresh grade.

Along with the letter, I submitted proofs that I had been diligent in completing all my assignments throughout the semester. Within a couple of days I got a response from the Dean's office informing me that my case would be reviewed at a special convening of the faculty of the School of Art, and that I would hear of their decision in two weeks. It was the longest two weeks I had ever experienced as I waited for my fate to unfold. The decision came to me in the mail. They deliberated and decided to give me a second chance. I was given three weeks to write the paper again.

I was triumphant! It was a defining moment in my life. For the first time I realized that it was up to me to take charge of my own destiny; it was okay to stand up and fight for what I believed in. I knew that I was going to be all right because I could count on myself even in the most hopeless situation. The event changed the way I looked at myself. I didn't have to be a victim. I didn't have to be that shy, timid person who had been taught to accept her fate. At that moment, I literally shed a layer of skin and became another person. The person that emerged was self-confident, self-reliant, and empowered. I could truly do anything I set my mind to do. My future was all up to me!

The words of William Earnest Henley's *Invictus* rang in my ear:

It matters not how straight the gate,
How charged with punishments the scroll,
I am the captain of my fate,
I am the master of my soul.

18
For All We Know

MOST OF THE girls who came to Barat had only one goal in mind: to find a well-to-do husband who would guarantee a life of comfort. Their education was intended to prepare them for the duties of a high society wife who would effortlessly oversee a beautiful home filled with artwork, expertly perform the duties of hosting dinners and parties, and capably preside over charity events and other acts of philanthropy. Their time in college was to give them maximum opportunities to meet that eligible husband.

Every week, social "mixers" were held in one of the three college dormitory buildings or the social room in the Old Main building. At least once a month buses came to Barat to take the girls to their boyfriends or boyfriend-hopefuls at Notre Dame. There were also organized carpools to go to the University of Chicago or Northwestern University campuses to attend the various and sundry social affairs. The goal was to find that perfect husband, and what better places to look than Notre Dame, Northwestern, and the University of Chicago?

That, however, was not my concern. I had totally different priorities, and none of them included having fun or looking for a husband. I never went to any mixers or on any husband-seeking field trips. I was focused on practical matters, such as getting through school and making sure that I had enough money to take care of myself. Every minute of every day was spent on either work or school. Every penny I earned went into my bank account.

It was the end of my first year in Barat. Everyone was busy with finals and term papers so that they could finish off the semester and go home for the summer break. It was my first summer in the United States and I had no place to go. The campus shut down for the summer so staying in the dorm was not an option. Desperately, I searched for a place to live for the summer.

I had befriended an older Chinese couple named Isaac and Emily who lived in town. They were devout Christians and went out of their way to provide friendship and support to the Chinese foreign students at Barat. Isaac was a librarian at Lake Forest College, and they lived with their two young children in a two-bedroom apartment provided by the college. I turned to Isaac and Emily for help. Isaac knew that he needed to help me or else I would end up being an unwanted guest in his small apartment. A co-worker was recently divorced, and she was taking in boarders to supplement her income. Isaac put me in touch with Mary, and she agreed to rent one of her rooms for $25 a week. The rent would be split between me and another boarder whom I had yet to meet.

I could afford my half of the rent, and I was happy to have found a place to live. When I got there, however, my roommate was a no-show. I told Mary that I couldn't afford the full weekly rent amount, but I really needed a place to stay. She felt sorry for me and told me that I could live in the basement for the $12.50 a week we had agreed on.

So I moved to the basement of my future mother-in-law's house in Lake Forest. It was an unfinished basement. The rafters on the ceilings were exposed and the floor was bare concrete. There were no bathrooms and no closets. An old worn mattress placed on the floor served as my bed and a rope strung between two posts became my wardrobe. But it was clean and dry, and I had free use of the kitchen and the bathroom upstairs. I was fine with the arrangement. I was happy to have a roof over my head.

That summer I met my future husband Andy, who was my landlady's son. He was the first American boy I met. Andy had boyish good looks with light brown hair and big brown eyes. He had a car, and he offered to take me around town. For the first time since I arrived in America, I finally went to downtown Chicago to see some of the sights and eat at nice restaurants. It was fun and exciting. It was also the first time that I experienced the attention of the opposite sex, and it stirred up a whole new set of feelings within me. Above all, it took away my loneliness and infused my dreary life with moments of happiness. At last, I had someone who was kind to me, someone I could talk to, someone who would actually care that I got up in the morning that day.

Andy's parents had divorced when he was a teenager. He was a loner and didn't have many friends. He worked the night shift as a ramp serviceman handling baggage for Eastern Airlines. The job suited his personality because he preferred to deal with luggage rather than people. He had chosen the graveyard shift so that he would be pretty much left alone.

Andy didn't get along with his mother. Mary was a tall, slender, elegant woman from a privileged family in Nebraska. She was raised to enter life as a socialite, and meeting Andy's dad Herb fulfilled that dream. Herb was a graduate of Northwestern University and a successful marketing executive with the J. Walter Thompson Company in Chicago. Thompson was known for its pioneering role in the development of the advertising industry. Herb was responsible for major accounts, including Oscar Meyer. They bought a house in Lake Forest and raised four children. Mary lived the life of an executive's wife, spending her time playing bridge, golf, and tennis, shopping and attending cocktail parties. She chain-smoked and loved her Manhattans. She drove a Cadillac and had a wardrobe of beautiful party dresses. I recall seeing a gorgeous yellow chiffon dress hanging in her closet with the price tag still on it, showing that it had cost over $200, a king's ransom for a dress in 1970.

But when Herb lost his job, the marriage quickly deteriorated and ended in divorce. Mary had to get a job. She ended up working in the Lake Forest College Library where she met my friend Isaac. Mary was a better socialite than a mother. Her four children all suffered from neglect. All the boys in the family had issues with their mother. When I met Andy, he was reclusive and antisocial. He owned two shirts, both bought from the Salvation Army, one with a big hole in the back.

Andy was fascinated with everything military and he had planned to leave home and sign up for the army soon after high school. Meeting me changed that plan.

That summer Andy and I fell in love. We were married two years after we met. We had no money. A generous minister at the Church of Lake Bluff graciously agreed to marry us for free. I wore a white prom dress with a green sash from J. C. Penney's. We spent sixty dollars on flowers. A college friend was our photographer. Mary hosted a light luncheon reception in her house.

Our wedding was attended by a handful of my friends from Barat. No member of my family came.

I had one semester left in college. I was twenty-two and Andy was twenty-one. We were two lonely souls who were drawn to each other out of desperation for love and family. Getting married was my idea. My Christian upbringing made me feel sinful at the mere thought of living together without being married. I also felt that I was indebted to Andy. He had been kind to me like no one else had been since I came to the States. Guilt was not a good reason to be married, as I later found out. We couldn't have been more different. We didn't want the same things in life. Our marriage was in trouble from the start. Our years together were filled with unhappiness. It ended in divorce twenty years later.

In hindsight, I realize that I was unfair to Andy. I knew almost from the start that I had married for the wrong reasons. The song that I had chosen to be sung at our wedding was The Carpenters' *For All We Know*. The wistful lyrics, "And love may grow, for all we know" betrayed what I already knew. I was not in love; I was hoping that love would grow over time.

19

No Place to Go but Up

IN EARLY 1973, I pounded the pavement for two months, applying for a job to every bank in downtown Chicago. It was a cold winter and a bitter, disappointing search.

After three and a half years of grueling hard work, I graduated from Barat College with a Bachelors Degree in Economics. In spite of working full-time, I managed to shave one semester from the four-year degree program. My dream was to sit on the Economic Board of Advisors in some high profile bank. But it was not to be. A downturn in the economy had caused jobs to be scarce.

I wanted to work for a bank because I thought that my degree in Economics would be directly relevant. On this January morning, I walked into one of the last Chicago banks I had on my list. I filled out the application and was immediately directed to a room to take a typing test.

For a woman looking for a job in the early 1970s, the first thing you had to do was to pass a typing test. I couldn't type to save my life, but I couldn't get an interview without taking the test. I took the test and nervously waited for my interview.

Sitting behind his sleek gray desk, the recruiter, a middle-aged man, broke the news to me. I didn't do well on the typing test. However, he did have a job for me. The job was to work in the mailroom sorting mail. My hours would be from 7 a.m. in the morning to 4 p.m. in the afternoon. The pay was minimum wage.

I was flushed with disappointment and humiliation. In an attempt to salvage my pride, I drummed up courage to ask what I thought was an intelligent question. "Will there be any promotional opportunities?"

He paused, cast a disdainful glance at me, and spoke condescendingly. "Honey, this is the lowest job in the company. There *is* no place to go but up."

I walked out of his office, my face hot and burning. My heart was pounding with humiliation and anger. I told myself that I was better than this. I hadn't come halfway around the world to be a mailroom clerk.

Yes, from this point on, there will be no place to go but up.

That day I opened the newspaper and went straight to the Help Wanted section of the Classified Ads. I searched for the jobs with the most advertised openings. I was looking for any job that would pay well, never mind that it had nothing to do with my education or what I wanted to do for a career. My goal was to get the job that companies were looking to fill and willing to pay. I noticed that two jobs were in great demand: accounting and computer programming. To be an accountant would require that I go back to school and get another degree. It would take too long. Computer programming was an emerging field. Very few schools offered Computer Science degrees at that time, so any programming training could open the door for me. Instantly I made my decision.

I took out a loan and enrolled at Control Data Institute (CDI), a trade school for computer operations. CDI was a typical trade school that was more interested in taking your money than giving you quality training. Everyone that came through their doors was tested for aptitude, and everyone was told that he or she would do well. Many came to CDI because the government was paying for it, mostly from the GI Bill or welfare benefits.

I took the accelerated Computer Programming class, which ran for only four months. The $2,500 in tuition was a hefty sum for such a short class. That didn't bother me. I knew it was just a stepping-stone. During those four months, I learned FORTRAN, BASIC, COBOL, and RPG. The classes were interesting but didn't have any depth. It wasn't hard to figure out that you couldn't become a programmer in four months. It was a calculated move on my part to open doors, and I would prove to be right.

The programming certificate added to my Bachelor's degree immediately transformed me into a sought-after candidate. When I graduated, I got four offers from the biggest Chicago companies. These included Arthur Anderson (later became Anderson Consulting), CNA Financial, and two insurance companies.

I chose CNA Financial because of its reputation for providing extensive training for computer programmers. During the interview, the recruiter boasted to me that many programmers called themselves alums of the "CNA University" because of the comprehensive training they got from CNA. I knew that it would be the right place to start my programming career.

In the early 1970s, Equal Employment Opportunity (EEO) was a huge initiative. The politics of gender had begun to play out on the American stage. Women were starting to enter the work force, and they quickly found that equity did not apply to gender. Women were usually the last to get jobs and the first to lose them. The disparity in pay and promotional opportunities was glaring. Yet few women felt it was their right to demand equal pay for equal work.

When I was hired by CNA, I was delighted to be given a salary of $8,800 a year, which was a living wage in 1973. I was thrilled until I found out that a male classmate of mine, who had exactly the same credentials I had, received a starting salary of $10,000 a year. Peter and I graduated from the same Computer Programming Certificate program at CDI. I was top of my class in the daytime program; Peter was the top of his class in the evening program. Peter had a Bachelor's degree in Chemistry. I had a Bachelor's degree in Economics. Besides our gender and racial differences (Peter was white), I saw nothing that would justify our difference in pay. Being young and naïve, my sense of fairness was violated. I marched into my manager's office and demanded an explanation.

My manager was very offended and told me that it was a management decision and that it was none of my business. I stayed exactly one year at CNA.

I was grateful to CNA, however, for launching my career in data processing. At CNA, I received training to be a mainframe programmer. Those were the early days of computing. Programming was in its nascent stage. At CNA, all the programming was done using punch cards. A cart would come around every afternoon and collect the batches of punch cards from each programmer. The punch cards were then processed by a mainframe computer overnight. The next day we got back a printout of the program. If it didn't work, we would make changes to the punch cards and try again. Since the turnaround time was only once a day, it took months to debug a simple program.

We had lots of leisure time on our hands. The men liked to play cards in the cafeteria. The ladies took long coffee breaks during the day and went on shopping excursions at lunch. The CNA Plaza, the bright red iconic building in the middle of the Chicago skyline, was centrally located in downtown Chicago. The building boasted of well-appointed facilities, including an executive dining room where I loved to dine on frog legs. The working atmosphere was very relaxed, and there was very little pressure from work. Life was good.

Shortly after I started working at CNA, I heard from one of my co-workers that she and her husband were buying a condominium called a quad. A quad was a style of townhouses popular in the 1970s and 1980s. Think of a square building divided into four quarters, each sharing two walls with the other units. These multiple unit dwellings shared the land, the grounds, and the common areas. They were very reasonably priced because of the shared ownership.

The subdivision that my co-worker was buying in was located in an up and coming neighborhood called Schaumburg about thirty miles northwest of Chicago. That weekend we drove out to Schaumburg to see what an affordable home in America looked like. The models all consisted of two bedrooms and one and a half baths. They were cheerfully decorated and furnished in the typical décor of the early 1970s. The walls were covered in silver foil wallpaper. The carpeting was yellow and green shag, and the appliances came in your choice of avocado or gold. I was in love. I wanted so much to have a house of my own. We had only $500 in the bank, but it didn't stop me. One of the lowest priced units had just become available because the buyer had backed out. The cost of the unit was $25,000. We only needed to put 5 percent down.

In the next three months, I saved like a maniac and came up with the $1,500 needed for the closing. The house was ours. We didn't need a moving truck because we had no furniture; only our sleeping bags, our clothes and some pots and pans. It was the start of my American Dream.

I bought my first piece of furniture: a green and yellow striped love seat that became the perfect centerpiece for my miniature living room. I loved the tubular steel frame design of the Wassily chair by designer Marcel Breuer and bought a pair of reproduction ones in chrome and vinyl. A chrome and glass coffee table from Montgomery Ward completed my ensemble. In our bedroom, I painted one wall a bold red color and hung a pair of paintings that were my own creation! I had copied the design of concentric red, white, and blue circles from a painting in our honeymoon hotel room. It was a striking graphic visual against the red wall and the navy bed cover. The result was a bright, cheerful, and modern apartment and my first successful attempt at interior design. I loved the results and I loved being a homeowner!

Our social life consisted of entertaining friends at home. We hosted small dinner parties and occasionally went out to dinner and movies. I tried my hand at cooking and got quite good at making American comfort food: meatloaf, baked chicken, spaghetti and meatballs, beef stew ... I didn't cook Chinese food because I didn't know how. Chinese cuisine had not yet arrived in America. Chinese food at the time consisted of Chop Suey, Subgum and Egg Fu Yung. There was neither inspiration nor ingredients to make real Chinese food.

Andy was working at Eastern Airlines on and off. He was let go once for sleeping on the job but was hired back with assistance from the labor union. Having graduated from Lake Forest College with a degree in History, there were few job options. I encouraged him to go back to school and take up studies in a more career-oriented field.

Why not teach? I pushed. When that didn't work out, I suggested law, and then accounting, programming, computer operations and on and on.

Over the next ten years, Andy went through numerous and varied curriculums only to quit each time shortly after he started. He didn't have the interest or the determination to complete anything. I was the one doing all the pushing. He went through the motions to placate me. I eventually realized that my dreams were not his dreams. He had never wanted a professional career. He had only wanted to be a soldier, and I had killed his dream.

Andy was a loner. He was happiest when he was in the basement building plastic model tanks, artillery, and fully landscaped battlegrounds. He loved reading history books and comic books. Looking back, I realize that he had the Peter Pan syndrome. He never wanted to grow up. Andy was also extremely anti-establishment. Every job he took, he got into arguments with the management. In his view, he was standing up for himself and other workers against the oppressive institution and its custodians. This cost him his job time and time again.

I was haunted by his inability to hold down a job. I can still recall nightmares of opening my eyes to find him standing there telling me that he had been fired. It threatened my innermost fears and insecurities. We fought constantly over money and his inability to contribute to the family's financial well-being.

Andy and I had very different dreams. He hated the rat race; I was driven to succeed. I wanted the great job, the nice house, the beautiful car, and the perfect vacations. I planned my every move to get what I wanted.

From the start, I had planned that I would job hop, at least for the first few jobs, to get the best pay. Eventually maybe I would settle down and really build a career. Incredibly, everything worked according to my very naïve plan!

My second job was at REA Express. REA Express stood for Railway Express of America. The company once operated the nation's largest ground and air express services, but poor management, strikes, and the pressure to stay competitive led to heavy losses, and the company slowly crumbled under its own weight. REA was on the brink of bankruptcy when I was hired. I didn't know and didn't care. All that mattered to me was the 35 percent pay raise I was offered.

The working conditions at REA were atrocious. Our office was located on Harrison Street, which was practically a slum in those days. Broken glass, dirt, and debris lined the streets. Vagrants and drunks were regulars at the doorsteps. Our office was on the second floor of a rundown building that housed the fleets of diesel fueled delivery trucks for REA Express.

Every day when we came to work, we had to clean off the layers of black soot that covered our desks. The noise of the trucks in the garage underneath our office space was deafening. The furnishings were stark and industrial. The bathrooms were filthy and dimly lit. I was the only female employee who dared to work there.

The transition from working at CNA to REA could be likened to the descent from heaven to hell. For most people it would have been too huge a culture shock, but not for me. I knew what I wanted, and I was being very pragmatic about it. I would soon meet someone just like me—someone who looked at life through such a practical lens that the dirt and filth at REA was nothing more than a minor annoyance.

It was at REA Express that I met my friend Sid and later his wife Joanne. Sid was a gifted programmer and a financial wizard. He was disciplined and very set in his ways. But he was also genuine and warm, and in time, he became a very good friend. Sid and Joanne were Jewish, but that didn't stop them from becoming a second family to my children as they were growing up. When I look back, I realize that my friendship with Sid and Joanne was the most valuable compensation I got out of REA Express.

Abruptly, less than a year after I started, my job came to an end. On a quiet Tuesday night in November of 1975, when I sat down to watch TV after dinner, I saw on the news that REA Express had filed for bankruptcy. In the next couple of weeks, news continued to pour in through the Teletype machine. Our salaries were immediately slashed by 10 percent. Then our payroll checks began to bounce. Still I stayed on to run the financial reports required by the financial audit that came with the bankruptcy proceedings. I even stayed at the Ramada Inn across from the office a few nights just to finish the reports. I paid those expenses out of my own pocket and was never compensated for it. It was my sense of duty that drove me to finish my job, even though what I really needed to do was to find a new job.

The search for a new job proved to be relatively easy. Within one week, I landed a job with A. B. Dick, a manufacturer of copiers and copy supplies. There was just one problem: I didn't own a car and didn't know how to drive. Getting from my home in Schaumburg to my new office in Niles, a suburb of Chicago, would be a problem since there was no public transportation. In order to start my job in three weeks, I had to learn to drive in three weeks!

So I bought a car, got behind the wheel, took my driver's license test, and found myself merging with rush hour traffic on the expressway in less than one month. At twenty-five, I became a first-time driver!

My new car was a fire-engine red Opal Manta. It was absolutely gorgeous. My driving skills, however, left a lot to be desired. The daily drive to work was a harrowing experience. As a newly licensed driver, I was extremely nervous. My palms would be sweating and my heart pounding as I navigated the expressways. I clutched the wheel so hard that my knuckles turned white. I kept my radio turned off, as I couldn't tolerate the slightest distraction. I was so tense the entire trip that my back would ache at the end of the day.

Traffic on the Kennedy Express was fast and unyielding. Large trucks and impatient rush-hour drivers dashed in and out of lanes. In the middle of this insanity was me, an inexperienced and terrified new driver, who hardly grasped the principles of how to change lanes. Many times, I just said a prayer and went. I was honked at all the time and narrowly escaped many near accidents.

My luck ran out on one cold February morning that first winter I started to drive. As I got off an exit ramp, I hit a patch of ice on an overpass. I panicked and slammed on the brakes. My car swerved and turned around 90 degrees, and when it finally came to a stop, I was blocking the opposite lane. I watched in horror as the cars from the oncoming traffic rushed towards me. A big Chevy hit me squarely on the passenger side. My glasses flew off and I saw splashes of blood on the dashboard. It happened so fast. I was in a state of shock. The police arrived followed by the ambulance. I was taken to the hospital. By a small miracle, I was only slightly injured. I had a big gash beneath my nose, suffered a fractured pinkie and cuts on my forehead and hands. After a couple of hours in the emergency room, I was released with only bandages. My car was not so lucky. It was totaled.

I replaced my beloved Manta with a second-hand copper colored Ford Mustang. I never really quite got over the accident. I am still today a nervous and timid driver, and I blame it on that fateful day in the winter of 1976 when but for the grace of God, I could easily have been killed or seriously injured.

At A. B. Dick, I learned very quickly that I was a mediocre computer programmer in a group of top-notch technologists. The Management Information Systems (MIS) team was young, bright, and talented. The team was led by Andrew "Flip" Filipowski, who later founded Platinum Technologies Inc. and went on to become one of the world's most successful technology entrepreneurs and industry visionaries. Looking back, I am amazed that Flip actually hired me after just a forty-five-minute interview. He offered me a starting annual salary of $15,000, a very generous salary for someone with barely two years of programming experience.

The late 1970s was the beginning of "online" programming. Up until then, programs were processed in the back room using gigantic mainframe computers, a process referred to as "batch programming." Bulky CRT monitors were just arriving on the scene. CRT stands for Cathode Ray Tube, describing the technology inside an analog computer monitor. The new wave of programming was to allow users to directly interact with the computer by entering and viewing information on the monitor. This was done via a new breed of programming languages, one of which was CICS. CICS (Customer Information Control System) was an online transaction-processing program from IBM. It required completely different syntax and programming concepts. CICS programmers were at the forefront of technology, and everyone wanted to be one.

I wanted to be a CICS programmer, but I also realized that there was little hope for me to be chosen to join the elite CICS team. I decided that I would find a way to rise above the crowd. For three months, I stayed after work and read all the manuals on CICS. Then I approached the department manager and requested to be assigned to the CICS team. I made my best pitch to convince him that I already knew the basics and was ready to jump in.

My bold move worked. It was an enormous risk, as I could fall flat on my face if I failed to learn quickly and deliver results. But the all-male CICS team welcomed me into their club. A couple of them took me under their wings and personally trained me. I had found a way to break out of mediocrity and became a member of the exalted online programming group.

Shortly after I started my job at A. B. Dick and less than two years after we bought our first home, we moved again. One day we were driving
down a long stretch of quiet road in a town called Hoffman Estates when I
saw a new subdivision looming out of the barren landscape. There were
four model homes perched in the foreground of what used to be an expansive piece of farmland. I pointed to the second house in the line-up and
proclaimed, "This is the house I want to live in!"

The house was a tri-level single family home with three bedrooms and
two baths. The asking price was $53,500 plus options and upgrades. It was
totally over our budget, but it didn't faze me. The house was a single-family
home—a house all to myself. It was to become the symbol of my American
Dream.

We picked the lot on a quiet cul-de-sac. We took no upgrades and no
options because we could afford neither. I prayed that the builder would
take a long time to finish the house so that we would have time to save
enough money for the closing. We moved into our perfect house with no
refrigerator or washer/dryer. We barely had $200 in the bank after we
closed. For months, we lived off a small dormitory-size refrigerator and
went to the laundromat. Living with the bare minimum didn't bother me.
The sacrifice was well worth it. I had *my own house*! It affirmed my need for
security and my sense of pride. It was proof that I had made it.

It was a very happy time for me. I threw myself into decorating and
landscaping. We put down tiles in the entry way and the kitchen. We built a
half bath in the lower level where the family room resided. We landscaped
the front yard, built a double-decker sun deck in the back, and planted
beautiful rose bushes and summer flowers.

I furnished the house with contemporary Scandinavian accents. For
the living room, we purchased a large camel colored sectional sofa, which
was inviting and comfortable. I mounted a large rust, brown, and tan color-
block rug on the wall to provide the perfect backdrop for the couch. For
the dining room, I purchased a beautiful honey-colored teak dining table
with a matching buffet. In the kitchen, we ate our meals around a sunny
butcher-block table with matching chairs. The house was everything I
dreamed it would be.

While I was working for A. B. Dick, I became a U.S. citizen. The date was May 1, 1977. A week prior, I was interviewed by an immigration and naturalization officer. I was asked to write, "Today is Wednesday" to prove my English competency. Some other question was asked, which I have long since forgotten, probably about who was the first president of the United States. At the swearing-in ceremony in Chicago's City Hall, I stood with two hundred other immigrants. We were from all parts of the world, in every shade of skin color, and from every walk of life. I felt like I was in a graduation ceremony. After we took the Oath of Allegiance, the hall broke out in applause and everyone hugged and greeted each other. After the ceremony, I received my Certificate of Naturalization. I was so proud to be a U.S. citizen at last. I finally felt a sense of belonging. Shortly afterwards I relinquished my Portuguese passport and applied for a U.S. passport.

I was doing well in my job at A. B. Dick. After joining the CICS team, my first project was to develop an online procurement system that was the first of its kind. I quickly became an integral part of the team. There was great camaraderie among the team members. We spent a lot of time together during and after work. Every Friday evening we went out for drinks and happy-hour at a local bar.

The team became my only social outlet. At home, Andy and I were becoming more and more distant, yet I didn't see the glaring red flags. I thought that was all anyone could expect out of a marriage. I thought most people lived in quiet desperation as I did. I thought I was supposed to be content with what I had.

Three years into my job at A. B. Dick, I got a call from a former boss to come to work for him in a company called Central Telephone Company (CENTEL). The job was for a Senior Programmer, and it came with a 14 percent salary increase. In spite of how much I liked my job at A. B. Dick, the mercenary in me saw nothing wrong with making the move. I changed jobs for the fourth time in five years.

Unlike A. B. Dick, CENTEL was a pedestrian MIS shop. The management team didn't have a technical background. There were many old guards from the telephone operations side of the business who were thrown into this new thing called Information Systems. It was difficult for this management team to grasp the concepts of computing, so they relied on ex-IBM employees who were hired as consultants. This was the beginning of the outsourcing trend. The consultants were paid outrageous salaries to deliver results that the management team was not able to deliver with its in-house staff.

My first assignment at CENTEL was to create an online order entry system for telephone services. The system was the first of its kind. I took advantage of the opportunity to learn from the best—the high-paid consultants—to build up my own expertise. At the project's completion, the team was recognized with an award in the form of a clear plastic cube desktop display that encased the first customer order. Very cool for 1978!

Then I moved on to work on the development of a new payroll system. CENTEL was a utility company that employed a highly unionized workforce. The challenge was to build into the system the flexibility to comply with the multitude of complex union rules and compensation policies. It was my first exposure to the impact that labor unions had on the American workforce.

As I got comfortable in my role, I saw the opportunity to get out in front. I approached Vonda, the group manager, with a bold proposal.

"We have so many consultants. What we need is internal leadership that can provide continuity in the department. I am the best CICS programmer you've got." I told Vonda. "If you make me the lead for the payroll project, you will not be sorry."

Vonda was an affable lady in her forties who had come from the operations side and had no technical background. She was an open-minded manager who was trying hard to be progressive. To my surprise, I convinced Vonda. She promoted me to be the programming lead.

I had an epiphany. I realized for the first time that people only saw what I allowed them to see. It was my job to show them who I was and what I could do. It became clear to me that I was a product like any other product on the market. As such, I must be able to differentiate myself and show my distinctive value. I should not expect to be rewarded just because I was sitting in a corner doing great work. This is a competitive world. In everything that I do, I must be able to "sell" the worth of my ideas or my abilities. All of these revelations were very counter-intuitive to my Asian brain.

I began to understand how to survive and get ahead in corporate America. There was no place to go but up.

20

Can You Have It All?

FOR A LONG time after we were married, I didn't want children. There were good reasons for how I felt.

Women were just beginning to enter the American work force in the 1970s and they wanted to be taken seriously. Getting pregnant sent out a signal to the contrary. I was doing well in my job. It looked like I was well on the path of getting somewhere in my career. Could I risk everything I had worked so hard for by getting pregnant?

Life was good. There was enough money to finally take away my perpetual financial worries. How would the expenses of raising a child change my life?

I was unhappy in my marriage. Would bringing a child into the marriage complicate things even more?

Six years into our marriage, my maternity instinct suddenly kicked in. Maybe it was the thought that a child would "fix" our marriage. Maybe it was my desperate need to have someone to love. The urge to be a mother grew increasingly strong. I couldn't wait for that chapter in my life to begin. I couldn't wait to be a mother.

In the spring of 1978, I was pregnant with Ryan. I had an average pregnancy. The morning sickness phase was mild and brief. I quickly put on a lot of weight. In those days, doctors encouraged mothers to put on a good amount of weight on the assumption that it was good for the baby. I gained over 35 pounds. I was 5' 1" and weighed 113 pounds before my pregnancy, so putting on 35 pounds was a big deal. In order for my legs to still reach the gas pedal, my stomach rubbed against the steering wheel, making it difficult to drive. My feet were swollen and I had the most painful case of hemorrhoids. I hated the taste of foods I used to love, like bacon and meat in general. Even the smell of cooking grease made me sick.

During the summer of my pregnancy with Ryan, my sister Amy, her husband Fred, and their four-year-old son Jerry came to visit. We had a wonderful time taking my nephew to museums, parks, and zoos. We played Mahjong and took long walks. It was the first time one of my family members had come to visit me, and it made me very happy.

Ryan Christopher was born on a cool autumn day in the October of 1978. I liked the name Ryan because it was a strong name. I also liked Christopher because I wanted my son to seek out adventures and embrace life. I gave Ryan the Chinese name of *Wei Yun* (偉仁), which phonetically sounds like Ryan and translates to *giving* and *caring*. My aspiration for my son was for him to grow up to be an honorable and loving human being and be loved by his family and friends. He fulfilled and exceeded every one of my expectations.

I was in love with my son the minute I laid eyes on him. Ryan didn't resemble Andy or me. He had an oval face, big brown eyes, strong eyebrows, and medium chestnut hair. His skin was fair and he looked completely Caucasian. To me he was perfection in a 7-pound 3-ounce package.

I had no family to help me when Ryan was born. Andy's mom lived about forty minutes away, but she never once offered help. My mother-in-law was not very maternal; she only saw her grandchildren on holidays and birthdays. The only friend I had was Joanne. On the day I came home from the hospital, Joanne came to the house and helped me sort out the baby's layette. As a new mother, I really missed my own mother and wished so much that she could be around to help me take my first steps as a mother.

I loved being a mother. I was so infatuated with my baby I couldn't put him down. I carried him in my arms everywhere I went. There were no laws requiring car seats at the time of Ryan's birth, or I would have been found in violation on so many occasions. At his slightest cry, I ran to him and picked him up.

Returning to work after Ryan was born was devastating. Daycare centers were just starting to spring up, but they didn't take infants. There was no paid maternity leave, so for financial reasons, I had to return to work quickly. I took five weeks off from work, during which time I frantically searched for a babysitter.

Virginia was my first babysitter. She lived in the same subdivision. She was Mexican and a mother of two adopted children. Her husband was a police officer. She adored Ryan the moment she saw him and we quickly became good friends. She taught me how to make Spanish rice and how to make instant coffee taste good by using condensed milk.

One day I came to pick Ryan up from Virginia. She was hiding the baby's face from me begging me not to be alarmed. Then she showed me a big gash over one of Ryan's eyebrows. She told me it was an accident, that Ryan fell and hit his head over the edge of the coffee table. More than being angry, I felt so guilty. I had left my baby with a stranger and he got hurt.

I made up my mind at that moment that I would find a job close to home so that I could get to my son whenever he needed me. One day I was casually glancing through job openings in the classified section of the *Chicago Tribune* when I came across an ad for Motorola. I had driven past this big campus with the sign Motorola on it many times on my way home. Even though I knew that Motorola was a big company, I had no idea what business it was involved in. The fact that it was only three miles from my house, however, made this an extremely desirable target for my next job.

The position was for a Project Leader for a new Payroll/Personnel system. I questioned whether I would qualify but I went ahead and applied. This was not the first time I had applied for a job at Motorola. A couple years prior, I had tried for a Senior Programmer position through a recruiter, but I was told that I was not technical enough. I decided there was nothing to lose but to try again. This time I was answering the ad directly, without going through an employment agency.

The manager who interviewed me was a young woman named Christina. Chris, as she liked to be called, was a vivacious woman with a broad smile and an infectious personality. She was smart, confident, and approachable. We hit it off right away. The interview went very well, so well that I got the call from Motorola a week later. Chris had offered me the job of Project Leader with a $30,000 starting salary. I was thirty years old when I accepted the job with Motorola. The salary was a good omen, not to mention a huge pay increase. My commute was reduced from forty to ten minutes. I couldn't have been happier.

So on July 14, 1980, I took my short drive to my fourth place of employment, Motorola, where I would stay for over thirty years.

Joining Motorola was a big change for me professionally. Coming from a small company, it was a massive leap to adjust to a company of almost one hundred thousand employees. My new job came with a steep learning curve. What I also didn't count on was the business travel. Motorola had three major payroll hubs: Schaumburg Illinois, Phoenix Arizona and Austin Texas. I was on the road every other month visiting the different payroll departments. Although I enjoyed the perks of business travel, I was not prepared for the guilt of leaving my young son at home. By then Andy was working night shifts as a computer operator, and on many occasions, I had to make overnight arrangements for Ryan. Leaving Ryan to the care of strangers tore me apart.

Yet I wanted another child. I felt it was important for Ryan to have siblings. Being an only child would be too lonesome. If my circumstance had been different, I would have had many more children. But for now, I wanted to have just one more.

As soon as Ryan was in pre-school, I tried for a second child. A couple of months later I had the feeling that something was happening to my body. Unable to contain my excitement, I bought a pregnancy test kit on my way to work and tested myself at work. The stick turned blue. I was so excited that I sought out my friend Trish and showed her the stick. Sadly, two months into the pregnancy I miscarried. I was devastated but not deterred. I ignored the doctor's advice to wait before conceiving again. While on a trip to Disneyland with Ryan in the spring of 1982, I found myself vomiting uncontrollably. I knew I was pregnant again.

I also knew right away that this baby would be a girl. The ultrasound tests in those days were neither reliable nor conclusive in determining gender, but I had the feeling. Blissfully, I started looking for a girl's name. I finally decided on the name Megan, which means *magnificent*. It also means Pearl, which I thought was so befitting for an Asian girl. For her Chinese name, I named her Yun Yun (欣欣), which means *Happy Happy*. There was nothing more that I wanted for my daughter than a life filled with joy and happiness.

Megan was a beautiful baby. She had brown almond-shaped eyes that hinted at being Asian. Her hair was very fine with golden highlights. She had a broad forehead, full cheeks, perfectly shaped ears and a delicate mouth. Her skin was fair like Ryan's. My baby girl weighed in at six pounds eight ounces.

Having a daughter gave me a great sense of completion. I called my mother from my hospital bed as soon as she was born. "I have a daughter," I told my mom. She was so happy for me. The circle of mother and daughter was complete. I knew how much I loved my mother; I now had a daughter of my own to love.

I got the "baby blues" right after Megan was born. Very little was known about *postpartum stress depression* in the early 1980s, so I wondered what was wrong with me. The depression was debilitating. I cried all the time. I had no energy to do anything. I felt constantly weighed down with anxiety and a deep sadness that couldn't be explained. I felt out of control. At work, even picking up the phone was a struggle. The guilt I felt at not having the interest and the energy to mother my children led me to suicidal thoughts. I felt overwhelmed with the demands of work and anxious about losing my job. That anxiety almost drove me to walk out of my job without considering the consequences.

The years of raising two young children while working to build a career were so challenging that most days it was a complete blur. I couldn't recall how the day began and how it ended. All I could do was to make it through one more day. Life was pure survival. It was putting one foot in front of the other and not quitting. I had no family around to help or give support. There was no relief for even a few hours. Somehow, I had to get through each day with little sleep and muster enough energy to be able to tackle the day after that.

Andy was a helpful father, but the responsibility ultimately fell on me. It probably had a lot to do with our personalities. I was a control freak. I needed things to be done right and on time. Andy was the complete opposite. He tended to let things slide and face the consequences later. I felt that if I wanted things to be done right, I had to do them myself. Even though I was in a marriage, I felt very much alone. I felt the constant pressure of all of the responsibilities: money, bills, childcare, housework, job …

My determination to give my children the very best drove us to move again, this time into the house of my dreams in Hawthorn Woods. The house was a French provincial style home with a soaring roofline. It was an all-brick rambling ranch sitting on over an acre of land. The subdivision was peppered with small ponds and massive trees. When I drove through the area and saw children swimming in the ponds, I was sold.

"My children will have the best childhood in this place," I told myself. It proved to be a poor choice.

I paid over $200,000 for the house, an extravagant sum in the mid-1980s. The house boasted over four thousand square feet. Every room was super-sized. There were three fireplaces, including an all-brick wood-burning one in the enormous country kitchen. The house even had two separate patios, one off the family room and another off the kitchen. It was a house built for entertaining. I felt that I had finally arrived.

The best part of the house was the full basement. It was so massive that my children learned to ride their bikes and roller-skate in the basement. At one time, I thought about putting in a bowling lane. Andy had his hobby corner all to himself in one far side of the basement. In another section of the basement, we painted a town square on the concrete floor complete with roadways and parks so that the children could drive their toy cars through town. It was indeed a magnificent dream home.

But the dream came with a price. With the big house and the big yard came big bills. Everything from the utilities to the property taxes was sky high. The maintenance, cleaning, and landscaping costs doubled from the last house we owned. The biggest downside that I didn't foresee was the isolation. Because all the houses in the township sat on an acre or more of land, my children had to be driven to friends' homes and to playgrounds. Worst of all, their schools were over seven miles from the house. It made attending school activities very challenging. My commute to work also went from four miles to eighteen and my driving time went up accordingly.

Ryan, who was outgoing and gregarious, had no problem making friends in the neighborhood. It also helped that he was allowed to walk by himself within the boundaries of the subdivision. Megan had a more difficult time. She had to be driven everywhere. One day I found her crying in her room.

"I am not happy here, Mommy," she sobbed. "I have no friends." It was an *Aha*-moment for me—a big house did not always make a happy home. We lived in our big house in Hawthorn Woods for eight years. I often wonder if I could have given my children a different set of childhood experiences had I not moved them to a lonely big house in a secluded neighborhood.

As the children got older, things gradually got easier. We fell into a routine. Weekends consisted of housework, yard work, and taking the children to their various lessons and activities: ballet, soccer, scouting, tennis, piano ... A hard-driven perfectionist, I tried to fit in as many family outings as possible—visiting museums, zoos, aquariums, nature trails ... I wanted my children to have a happy childhood and memorable experiences. It was never too much work to be a family.

One of our favorite things to do was to take the children to museums. There were so many great museums in Chicago, but the Museum of Science and Industry was our absolute favorite. Ryan loved the interactive displays and hands-on learning. Once we were inside the museum, every handset must be picked up, every display must be touched, and every button must be pushed. It was fun and educational at the same time. First stop was the hatchery, where we hung around and watched the chicks hatch. Another must-see was the human fetuses in various stages of gestation exhibited in glass encasements. Ryan and Megan marveled at the human likeness of the fetuses, not quite grasping the fact that these were real human babies who had never had the chance to be born. Other favorite stops included the dollhouse, the miniature model town with the wrap-around train, the underground mine, and the World War II German submarine. The Museum of Science and Industry was such a gift to the children of Chicago. It was an important part of my children's growing up.

We were season ticket holders to the Museum's Omnimax Theater and saw almost every show ever played there. This was Chicago's only five-story stadium-seating theater that gave the viewers the experience of being immersed in the film. Unforgettable shows I watched with my children included "The History of Flying," beginning with the Wright Brothers through the space program; "Fire" from the days of the caveman to the power of the volcanoes; "The Living Sea," which showcased the wonders of deep-sea explorations; and "Everest," which told the dramatic true story of the successful ascent of Mount Everest—a story of finding hope, strength, and triumph in the wake of tragedy.

I loved every one of the shows we saw. I cherish the memories of watching these shows with my children. I believe they not only served to entertain and educate, but also made a lasting impact on my children's character, outlook, and aspirations.

I loved celebrating my children's birthdays. What I didn't love was the American ritual of children's birthday parties. I just didn't like the more-of-everything culture. When the children were little, it was fun having small parties at home and having cake, ice cream, and pinning the tail on the donkey. As they got older, they were invited to their friends' parties. Soon the whole first-grade class had to be invited to Chuck-E-Cheese or Showbiz Pizza. Later it was going to Great America and hosting a Make-a-Bear party. I was convinced that the birthday-party arms race was designed to add more stress to the already overwrought working mom. I wracked my brain thinking of the next birthday-party thing to do. Thank goodness I am not raising young children today, as I see that it is even more out of control. I understand that it has gone beyond clowns and magicians to bringing in zoo animals, Disney characters, face painters, and caterers. I believe this fuels the all-about-me culture and puts unnecessary stress on mothers and the family budget. But then again, I am very Chinese!

Summer vacations were especially important to me. I knew my children would grow up quickly. There was an urgency to collect wonderful experiences. I spent hours planning and booking travel arrangements every year to make sure that we had an exciting destination to look forward to. Over the years, we took our children to Hong Kong and Macau, Disneyland and Disney World, Phoenix and San Francisco, and drivable destinations such as Myrtle Beach South Carolina, Turkey Run Indiana, Door County Wisconsin, and the Wisconsin Dells. We even went on a Caribbean cruise when they were teenagers. Today these destinations may not seem like a big deal, but in the 1980s and 1990s, we felt extremely privileged to be able to afford these vacation extravaganzas. For me, it was worth every penny to create happy childhood memories for my children.

As I think about those years, I find myself returning to the question, *Can you have it all?* Many career women in my day chose not to have children. There were many reasons, but I know that one of those reasons was that it interfered with their professional aspirations.

In the 1970s, women were just starting to enter the workforce and learning how to fit into the American working scene. Women with high professional aspirations worried about being seen as not serious about their careers if they got pregnant. Companies were not accommodating of working mothers. When Ryan was born, there was no paid leave for childbirth. My bosses were not sympathetic if I had to leave a meeting early because I had to pick up my child before the daycare facility closed. At the office, women avoided talking about their children lest they be considered too maternal and therefore not serious professionals.

Mothers were judged by whether or not they stayed home. When I got pregnant, my colleagues asked me, "You are *NOT* coming back to work, are you?" Conventional belief was that good mothers stayed home with their children. There was always the pressure of choosing between family and career.

So, when I think back on juggling a career and family, I ask myself, was it all worth it? For me, the answer is a resounding YES. It was a personal choice, but it also had a lot to do with my personality. I truly believe that if I had been a stay-at-home mother, I would have been under-challenged and under-fulfilled. I probably would have doubted my own self-worth. With all that baggage, I wonder how good a mother I could have been. Knowing me, spending every day and night with my children would have invoked the law of diminishing returns. As it was, by the time I got home from work, I was so thrilled to see my children that I made an extra effort to spend quality time with them.

Is daycare bad for the children? My children grew up in daycare. They had good days and bad days, just like any other children. They were probably subject to more colds and other ailments, but I think they also built immunities earlier. The socialization aspects, I believe, were invaluable. They learned how to behave in a group setting and to share and take turns.

I also think that having structure is good for children. In daycare, there are daily routines and schedules. The children know what to expect. These are all positives in my book.

How do you balance work and children? I did it with lots of planning and by being flexible and creative. When I knew that I would miss one of Megan's school performances, I would ask the teacher if I could come for the rehearsal. When I had to make a recruiting trip to Illinois State University, I brought Ryan with me. He helped me hand out cookies and business cards. We had a great mother and son bonding time. Ryan still remembers the trip to this day. When I had to do work at home, I tried making a game out of my work. While rehearsing my presentations I would sit them across the dining room table and asked for their feedback. They felt important and grown-up!

Speaking for me, there is no question that being a working mother was worth every measure of sacrifice and every ounce of hard work. Being a mother fulfilled me in a way that no job or career ever could. Raising my children gave me so much joy. Through my children's eyes, I saw the wonder of childhood sparkle anew. Being able to shape and mold their young lives was like being given a second chance to redo my own growing up. On the other hand, having a career gave me real balance and true fulfillment. My job challenged me to grow as a person. Being a working mom gave me an identity beyond that of being Ryan and Megan's mother. I got the chance to figure out who I was and to grow into the person that I was proud to become.

Being a working mother was not a choice that I made. It was a necessity, but it turned out to be the best thing that happened to my children and me. I am fortunate that I got the best of both worlds and that my job actually made me a better mother.

21

Being a Chinese Mom

ARE CHILDREN BORN to immigrant parents first-generation children or are they second-generation immigrants? No matter how they are labeled, one fact is clear: My children, not by their choice, have inherited two disparate cultures: Chinese by blood, American by birth.

As the immigrant parent to my American-born children, I stumbled through the process, having received absolutely no training or instructions whatsoever for such a role. I wasn't prepared for the perils of raising kids in America nor did I give much thought to which is the better parenting method—the American way or the Chinese way, which by now are well known to be stereotypically different.

Most of us raise our children the way we were raised. *Five thousand years of Chinese history can't all be wrong.* So why wouldn't I follow all the methods of raising successful Chinese children handed down through the generations?

Because my instincts told me differently. I didn't like how *success* is being defined in traditional Chinese terms—over-achieving and making lots of money. I didn't agree with all the methods designed to raise successful children that have been revered throughout Chinese history. For me the price to be paid is often too high, especially when passion, creativity, self-worth ... are sacrificed in the name of success. I value my children's happiness above all.

On the other hand, I whole-heartedly believe in hard work and in living a productive life. I see great beauty in the Chinese philosophy of respect for parents and love for family. I want these values to be my children's Chinese heritage.

So I set out to find my own way. My goal was to take the best of both worlds—Chinese and American parenting methods, and strike the right balance. I didn't always achieve the perfect balance. Oftentimes I found myself conflicted, and I may have been wishy-washy, even. But always I followed my heart and my instincts.

I set the following standards for my children:

- Your priority is to study hard and get good grades. You are expected to enter a good university and be prepared with life skills to enter this increasingly competitive world.
- Don't take the easy way out. Always do your best to meet the challenge. Put in extra effort in everything that you do, such as earning extra-credit in schoolwork or going for advanced placement classes. Extra effort is what builds character.
- Learn that money doesn't grow on trees or come from ATMs. It takes hard work to earn money.
- Only spend what you can afford. If you make a dollar, put twenty cents away. It's fun to set goals for what you want to buy. When you can buy what you want with money you've earned yourself, you'll feel proud.
- Honor your parents. Always show respect and gratitude to those who love you and who sacrifice for you. This is the Chinese concept of "filial piety" (devotion to parents).
- Be humble and appreciative. Know the difference between being egotistical and being self-confident.
- Enjoy your childhood. Try a lot of things and have a lot of fun. You're only a kid once.

What I didn't do, however, was to demand that my children get straight A's in school or win first honors in competitions. I don't hurt my children's self-esteem by degrading them verbally or physically, ever. When

I was a child, it was common for parents to use punishment and belittling as a way of motivating children to do better. Parents didn't shy away from hurtful words or physical punishment. Chinese children who are strong and gifted are able to rise above the berating, insults, and punishments to grow up to be over-achievers, reinforcing the stereotype of Chinese being super-smart and accomplished. Unfortunately, children who are more sensitive or less gifted succumb to the insults they hear, leading to resentment and self-doubt. I personally know individuals who led a life of despair and bitterness and who even attempted suicide because of this model of parenting.

Like most American parents, I believe in encouragement and support. I am extremely generous in giving praise to reinforce positive behavior. Words such as *I know you can do it … I'm so proud of you …* are lavished on my children at every opportunity. Even more important, when they failed to win a competition or make it into a team, I made sure that I was there to comfort and encourage. A child needs to know that he is loved unconditionally, regardless of his achievements.

Another tenet of my parenting approach is to ensure that my children build confidence and self-reliance. I fought against my own lack of confidence all my life. I wanted to give my children a strong sense of themselves and to trust in their own abilities to make the right choices. For that reason, I gave them lots of freedom—be it the choice of clothing or bedroom décor, choice of music or sports activities, or what TV programs or movies to watch. I had no strict house rules and very few do's and don'ts. I wanted them to learn to be self-governing because they won't be living under my watch forever.

Work ethics is another aspect of character-building that is important to me. Like most Chinese parents, I started Ryan and Megan on piano lessons when they were little. This seemed a very stereotypical thing for an Asian parent to do, and maybe I did fall for the stereotype after all. But I was honestly convinced that piano-playing would help the development of their eye-hand coordination and that musicality would lead to improved Math and cognitive skills. Also, I liked the discipline and perseverance aspects of playing a musical instrument. I am a believer that succeeding in something that requires grueling practice, focus, and willpower builds self-esteem.

My children didn't go to Chinese classes. To be clear, there were no Chinese classes in our neighborhood when they were growing up. Suburban Chicago didn't have a big Chinese population in the 1980's. I didn't have many Chinese friends; in fact, almost none at all for the first twenty years I was in America. I married white. The truth is, teaching a child a language in a home where only one parent speaks the language is hard, if not impossible. If I had the resources, I would have given my children the chance to learn Mandarin in a heartbeat, primarily because I believe that language is enriching, and what better language to learn than one that relates to your heritage? So maybe I will start with the next generation—my grandkids.

So what's it like to be my children? You should ask Ryan and Megan, but here's what I think they'll say:

Mom didn't teach us to speak or write Chinese, but we know how to order dim sum in Chinese restaurants. Har-kau, Shui-mei, Chuan-fun … We thought that's all Mom ever wanted us to do. *Why then is she trying so hard to teach Avery* (my granddaughter) *Chinese?*

Mom is erratic when it comes to Chinese customs and traditions. On Chinese New Year we always get *Lei See* (lucky money in a red envelope) and Peking duck for dinner if we are lucky. But then we don't celebrate any other Chinese holidays.

Mom's a good cook. We love her American Meatloaf and Pork Chops, but she also makes awesome Fried Rice and Egg Rolls. She has no luck though, trying to convince us that Fish heads and Chicken feet are delicacies. We are happy to let her eat all that good stuff.

We tune Mom out when she starts ranting in Cantonese. *Blah, blah, blah … blah blah, blah, blah.* We laugh at her and call her "the foreign woman", good-naturedly, of course. But Megan does get mad when Mom tells her in Cantonese "Don't be *Sil Hay!*" She knows that it means "Don't be so overly-sensitive!"

Mom likes to use funny Chinese idioms like *The Old Farmer Who Lost His Horse*. The message is about the fleetingness of fortunes: bad things that happen can become blessings, and good fortune can be taken away in the blink of an eye. We get it—but *what does that have to do with us?*

Mom made us play piano when we were little. She thinks that all good Chinese parents make their children play piano or violin.

As soon as we were old enough, Mom signed Ryan up for soccer and Megan for Brownies. She thinks that all good American parents make their children play soccer and join the scouts.

Mom didn't expect us to do chores, but she did teach us to sew on our own buttons because she is convinced that it's a basic life skill.

Mom made us get part-time jobs as soon as we turn sixteen. She believed that it would teach us about the value of money. It worked, but not in the way she thought. Working in retail surely convinced us that we better study hard and get a cushy office job, because we would never want to spend the rest of our lives working in Best Buy or Imaginarium.

We have strange rituals in our family. On our birthdays, we have to offer Mom freshly brewed tea. Of course we get the message—that birthdays are not just about us getting lots of presents (which we like a lot), but it's also a time to show gratitude to those who love and nurture us. Still it's a strange custom, one that we're sure no other family practices. Megan likes to poke fun at the ritual. "Thank you, Mom, for giving me life," as she shoves the tea in front of Mom with a grand gesture and a big grin.

By the time we were old enough to handle a frying pan, Mom invented another ritual. This time it was to teach us patience. On Christmas mornings, before opening presents, we had to get up early and make breakfast for the family. It was actually fun making pancakes, scrambled eggs and sausages, and sitting down to a feast that we made ourselves, though it was a lot more fun ripping into our Christmas presents as soon as we finished eating.

It's important to Mom that we don't forget we are part Chinese when we are in front of the world. For our weddings, she custom-made traditional Chinese gowns to wear for the occasion. We also incorporated the Chinese Tea ceremony into our weddings. We knew it would make her happy.

Now that we are grown, we have lunch dates with our Mom ...

Ah, lunch dates with my children. It's all about communications. Communications is the lever to my parenting. I like to ask my children out to lunch because it gives us private time to visit with each other. On these occasions I learn what is really going on in their lives—their challenges and accomplishments, their hopes and dreams. It allows me to provide encouragement, offer comfort, and give advice. Through the years, having a solid connection with my children has been the most rewarding experience. It is what makes my job as a mother the best in the whole wide world!

I don't want my children to forget they are part Chinese but I also want them to be fully integrated Americans. I am ecstatic that my children turned out to be everything I hoped they would be. They have learned Chinese values but they also inherited the American spirit. Best of all, there is a strong bond of love and respect between us. When I see that my children are happy, healthy, and living a productive life, I know I have done something right.

My parents never taught me to hug. In America, I learned to open my arms and embrace my children.

Part Three

The Horse in the Wilderness:
My Audacious Motorola Journey

22

On the Shoulders of Remarkable Women

THROUGHOUT THE UNCERTAINTIES and changes in my life, there was one thing that gave me stability and security: my job at Motorola. This chapter is dedicated to my long and remarkable thirty-one year career at Motorola, and especially to the remarkable Motorola women in my life.

When I was hired by Motorola in 1980, I had no idea who Motorola was. The company had just moved its headquarters from the west side of Chicago to a sprawling campus in the suburb of Schaumburg. It had also just gone through a makeover, having sold off all of its consumer business (Motorola used to make home radios, car radios, and televisions!) to focus on a new one: handheld two-way radios. This was the beginning of the wireless communications era, and Motorola was at the forefront. It's a little known fact that in 1969, Neil Armstrong spoke the famous words "one small step for man, one giant leap for mankind" from the moon on a Motorola transceiver. In fact, the Federal Communications Commission (FCC) nicknamed the wireless frequency plan "the Motorola plan" because of the company's pioneering efforts. Motorola in 1980 employed over ninety thousand domestic employees.

Taking the job at Motorola was a no-brainer. I was offered a handsome salary and the title of Project Leader. My commute was not only dramatically reduced but the driving would be all local. For the first time in my career, I had my own office! It was a small 8' by 10' inside office, but it made me feel so important. I joined a department of four, three of whom were women. We were all project leaders and systems analysts for different financial systems projects.

I was hired to lead the development of a new computer system to pay Motorola's employees and calculate their payroll benefits. Two years prior the company had purchased an off-the-shelf solution, but the system never worked, so it was scrubbed. The decision was made to develop a solution in-house, and from scratch. My job was to define what the new system would need to do. To do that I had to work with the MIS (Management Information Systems, called IT today), Payroll, Tax, and Human Resource departments to figure out how the new system would work.

How do you do that? I had no idea. I had over-exaggerated my experience at the interview because I really wanted the job. Now it was time to pay the piper.

In the beginning, I had panic attacks on a daily basis. As the Project Leader, I was thrown into a setting where I had to conduct large corporate meetings and lead discussions. I had no such experience. At my first user meeting, I was so nervous that I had to leave the room to vomit in the bathroom. But I pulled myself together and came back to the meeting looking cool and collected. I told myself *don't let them see you sweat* as I went on with the charade that I knew exactly what I was doing.

So I set off to make myself into a Systems Analyst and a Project Leader. I taught myself to organize meetings, interview users, analyze operating procedures, and extrapolate system requirements. In meetings, I listened intently for facts and I studied behaviors. I summoned my best people skills to reach out across departments to build consensus. Slowly the pages of a systems requirements book in a three-ring binder emerged. It would become the foundation on which the new payroll system would be built. Two and a half years after I was hired, the first payroll check was printed from the spanking new Motorola payroll system that I was instrumental in designing!

My manager Chris was a huge fan. She somehow got the idea that I was brilliant in my job. She promoted me to Project Manager after only nine months.

At Motorola, Chris was an anomaly. The finance department in the 1980s was a good old boys club filled with middle-aged, over-bearing, conservative white males. Chris was a tall, vivacious, single white woman who was smart, outspoken, and self-confident. Her credentials included degrees from University of Chicago and Northwestern University, and she had prior consulting experience from the elite accounting firm of Deloitte and Touche. Her management style was collaborative. She was not afraid to speak her mind. She was the first female role model that I wanted to emulate.

It was easy to understand why some of Chris' peers were threatened by her fearlessness and independence. She would not allow herself to be side-lined when important projects and meetings were in the works. Instead, Chris would invite herself to meetings and poke her nose into projects where she thought she could make a contribution. That created enemies for Chris. She was stereotyped as being too bold, too pushy, and too aggressive. A year after I was hired, Chris left Motorola.

After Chris left, a new manager was hired to replace her. His name was Tim. Tim was a corporate ladder climber who didn't mind trampling on people on his way up. Not surprisingly, he took credit for my work repeat-edly. One time I completed a study on the computer system we would use for the Motorola Foundation, the philanthropic organization founded in 1953 to promote education in math and sciences. He was so impressed with my work that he told me, "I'm going to showcase you!" What happened next taught me a huge lesson. A couple of weeks later he issued the report in his name with some minor changes. I learned that I needed to toot my own horn. I would not ever again rely on someone else to "showcase" me.

Tim was a chauvinist. He once wrote in my performance review, "You're a woman first before you are a professional." To this day, I don't understand what that meant. Is being a woman a sign of weakness? Sure women are different from men. We tend to have more empathy, to show more emotions, to wear our feelings on our sleeves. To some men, this is perceived as weakness. Years later, after my divorce, another male manager remarked to me that Motorola considered divorced employees unstable. This obviously had to do with my gender. Women without a husband were seen as not having financial and emotional backing and therefore lacking in stability. Men, however, didn't suffer from the same stigma. It was a double standard.

The chauvinistic attitudes in Motorola's finance department never bothered Sandy. Sandy was one of my co-workers who also worked for Chris. She had a happy-go-lucky fun-loving personality that allowed her to not sweat the small things. She had two children close to my children's age so we had a lot in common. We quickly became fast friends.

Sandy showed me how to have fun. Because we were both working on the payroll project, we became travel buddies. Every other week we made our trip to Phoenix, which was Motorola's main payroll hub. The Double Tree Hotel became our home away from home. Sandy knew everyone in the payroll and personnel departments, so we often went out in a large group. We dined at hip local restaurants and danced at discos and night-clubs. I watched country dancing for the first time at the "No necktie" Pinnacle Peak Steakhouse. We enjoyed fabulous Mexican food at Los Olivos and Garcia's. I tasted my first Alaskan king crab-legs at the Pacific Seafood Company in Scottsdale.

We took driving trips on days when we could take off. One time we almost crashed a company car when we drove up an unpaved mountain trail called the Dead Man's Trail. On another occasion we took a daredevil drive in a sports car barely holding on to both car doors that would not close (we had messed up the doors). Sandy brought me out of my shell and taught me how to loosen up. Even though we had very different personalities and outlooks on life, I admired Sandy for her free spirit and the way she lived her life with joy and gusto.

After I completed the payroll project, I was given the responsibility of managing the Corporate Briefing Room Charts system. This was the computer system that generated the all-important monthly company financial overviews for the purview of Motorola's executive management. Numbers were crunched to produce summary information on budgeted versus actual sales and costs, and the future outlook based on orders, backlog, and so on. Graphs and charts were designed to give a bird's-eye-view perspective on the company's financial standing. All very boring stuff, but they were important tools for the company's executives to steer the company and make strategic decisions.

The system was programmed using a fourth-generation language called Nomad, a natural programming language that was among the first of its kind. Nomad was a non-procedural language designed for fast prototyping. I was trained as a COBOL programmer and had no exposure to avant-garde programming languages, which required a new way of thinking.

Lucky for me, I had a wonderful teacher by the name of Nadine. Beauty and generosity are the attributes that come to mind when I think of Nadine. She was an extremely talented programmer who taught me every-thing I knew about Nomad. It didn't take long for us to become good friends.

Nadine also taught me about poise and grace in the face of adversities. She and her husband Darrell tried for a long time to have a child, and she finally conceived after a long ordeal with fertility treatments. When she gave birth to her little boy Bradley, she was overjoyed. Many more fertility treat-ments thereafter, however, didn't yield a sibling for Bradley. Nonetheless, Nadine never complained about the struggles she went through, but was always grateful that she was able to realize her dream of becoming a mother.

During my ninth year with Motorola, both Sandy and Nadine left. Sandy moved to New Jersey and Nadine to Virginia, both on account of their husband's new employment. They remained the only female friends I made at Motorola.

Over the years, I kept in touch with both Sandy and Nadine. They both came to my wedding in 2003. Sadly, that would be the last time I saw Nadine. Some years later, I received an unexpected email from Darrell.

Joanna,

I was sorting through some of Nadine's collections of things, when I came across a letter from July 2003 from you with a picture from your wedding—and this email address.

I'm not sure when the last time was that Nadine spoke to you, but in November 2004 she was diagnosed with brain cancer and passed away October 24 (2005). I didn't have any way of getting in touch with any of her Motorola friends.

I'd be happy to fill you in.

Darrell

Nadine's premature passing shook me to the core. I called Darrell and listened with unrepressed grief and admiration for how she bravely fought her illness to the end. She kept her sense of humor and her graciousness in the darkest moments of her life. Nadine made me realize how fleeting life is. I will never forget my beautiful friend!

About fifteen years into my Motorola career, I crossed paths with another remarkable woman, Janiece, who made a lasting impact on my career.

I met Janiece while sitting next to her on a plane to Australia. We were traveling to Motorola's Melbourne office for different reasons and happened to take the same flight. I didn't know who she was, but quickly learned that she held a very powerful position at Motorola. We related to each other as women first. Janiece was in love. She had just met a guy at a garage sale. She was head over heels. She could hardly contain her excitement when she told me the story of how her neighbors, an elderly couple who watched her house for her while she was away, had called to report that some guy had come by to shovel her driveway. That guy would turn out to be her future husband, Tim.

Janiece started her career with Motorola in the production line. Her meteoritic rise to one of the highest positions in Motorola, that of Senior Vice President, was nothing less than a Cinderella story. But it was no accident. Janiece was visionary, driven, gutsy, outspoken, and tough. At the pinnacle of her career, she was recognized by the media as one of the most powerful woman in telecommunications.

Mao Zedong wrote in his little red book, "Women hold up half of the sky." This could be a Chinese proverb, or it could be something that Mao used as a slogan and propaganda, but I loved the symbolism. Unfortunately, in my career I didn't always see equal opportunities and equal treatment for women. My experience had been that men set the norms that women had to follow. To challenge the status quo and break the proverbial glass ceiling, a woman had to behave like her male counterparts.

What was remarkable about Janiece was not how successful she became or how high she climbed the corporate ladder. It was the fact that she dared to be a woman even as she fought to be successful in the male-dominated, management-by-fear corporate culture of her era. Janiece never compromised who she was. She was caring, nurturing, and compassionate.

She didn't try to emulate her male peers in her style, the way she dressed, or the way she conducted herself. She had a presence that commanded attention and respect, even though it was decidedly feminine. I saw Janiece as the "Oprah Winfrey" of Motorola. Like Oprah, Janiece mentored many, but her biggest impact was on the women whose lives she touched.

When Janiece found out that I was a mentor to young women professionals in Motorola, she nominated me to receive the "Woman of Achievement" award from the Girl Scouts of America. The award was given to women who the organization recognizes as great role models for young women. It was a great honor. My children came to my award ceremony. In my acceptance speech, I spoke of my mother and how she made sure that we had money to pay tuition before we bought food, and how education helped me to get to where I was. The audience was moved to tears. I was so proud that my children were there to witness the recognition I received.

Janiece was my finest professional female role model. She showed me that you didn't have to behave like a man to be successful in the corporate world. She gave me the visual for what a strong female executive looked like and behaved like. I saw by her example that toughness was not synonymous with aggressiveness, and that getting results didn't have to conflict with being caring and compassionate and having respect for people and their dignity.

We all have heroes in our lives. Chris, Nadine, Sandy, and Janiece were my heroes. They were also my teachers. From Chris, I learned to be fearless. From Nadine, I learned generosity and grace. From Sandy, I learned how to live life fully. From Janiece, I gained the courage to be myself.

The strength I have today and the character I have built came from the people in my life who touched me in some way. I want to let them know that their impact did not go unnoticed. Standing on the shoulders of remarkable people, one can certainly see a lot farther.

23

A Battle of Two Cultures

"PLEASE HAVE A seat."
"No, thank you. I'm just fine standing."

"Please go ahead."
"No, you first."

"Would you like some tea?"
"No, please don't go through the trouble."

"This meal looks wonderful."
"You probably won't like it. I'm not a very good cook."

"Your son is so smart."
"No, he really isn't. He should do better."

The Japanese have a word for this behavior. The word *enryo* (遠慮) de-
scribes so well the cultural expectation imposed on many Asians, especially
Asian women. *Enryo* means to avoid conflict through self-restraint and con-
sideration for others. It is a form of reserve and humility that is highly valued among Asians. The notion is that in order to live harmoniously with
others, one should avoid imposing one's own preferences or opinions on

them. It follows that it is not acceptable to show any form of aggression in social situations. It is especially not acceptable to openly contradict a person in a position of authority. The practice even extends to belittling of oneself, one's success, or one's possessions so that others don't feel inadequate.

This was the way I was raised—to be humble, reserved, and self-effacing. The conflict becomes clear when you contrast this kind of behavior with the behavioral norms in Corporate America.

- The Asian is raised to avoid eye contact with strangers so as not to show aggression. For the American, eye contact shows self-confidence.
- The Asian doesn't want to make any waves by taking the first action. The American admires and rewards initiative taking.
- The Asian is taught to talk only when addressed. To the American, if you don't say anything, it shows that you have no opinion.
- The Asian avoids confrontation at all cost. The American debates, argues, and defends his opinion as his right.
- The Asian refrains from personal contact when meeting strangers. The American wants to show friendliness and openness through handshake and embrace.

In my view, this is part of our social conditioning and there is no right or wrong between these attitudes and behaviors. However, these behaviors only work in the setting that promotes them. When taken outside of those settings, they become ineffective and confusing.

For example, when I was given an assignment, the first thing I did was to express doubt in my ability to perform the job. It was my way of showing humility. My intention was to under-promise but over-deliver. The Asian listener knew that he was supposed to disregard these self-effacing remarks, but in the American culture, such humility made me look weak. I came across as lacking in self-confidence.

As Chinese children, we were taught to be courteous and wait our turn to speak. "You first" or "After you" was the etiquette drilled into our behavior. Americans don't understand this kind of behavior. In American-style meetings, if you wait your turn to speak, you will never get the chance to say anything. Americans tend to dominate discussions, as they are highly competitive in their communication style. In order to be heard, you must jump in as soon as the other speaker pauses. This is extremely difficult for an Asian who wants to take time to think through his ideas thoroughly before he speaks, and who thinks it is discourteous (and it is) to cut other people off before they could complete their arguments.

Another challenge for me was accepting praise. As a child, I was taught to be modest and to reject compliments or praise, and this carried over into adulthood.

I have a Chinese neighbor named Ming who has a four-year-old daughter named Megan. Ming was an immigrant but her daughter was born in the United States. One day I saw Megan wearing a new dress and I told her she looked pretty. Megan smiled and said, "Thank you." Ming became visibly upset with Megan. "No, no, no, Megan. You can't say that. Tell Mrs. Joanna that you don't think you are pretty."

And that was exactly my problem. Just like Ming, my mother taught me to reject any compliments lest I became too immodest. During performance reviews, for example, I felt the constant urge to reject my boss' praises and often offered to point out my weaknesses. This self-degrading behavior invariably worked against me, as my boss usually ended up agreeing with my negative self-critique. If I didn't believe in myself, why should he?

I had to keep reminding myself that it was okay to take credit and accept compliments that I had earned. When I was given a challenge, I learned to show enthusiasm and confidence in my ability to do the job. In meetings, I learned to look for those opportune moments to interject, especially when I was among people who wanted to dominate the conversation.

In the early days of my career, my language skills also worked against me. One day a callous manager made the remark, "When you speak, it raises the hairs on people's necks!"

What does that mean? I was criticized for being too direct, too blunt—that I lacked tact and polish in my spoken English. The comment was biting and hurtful. I dismissed it as one that came from an ugly American who lacked cultural sensitivity. But later I came to a new understanding. For those of us who are foreign-born and still struggling to master the nuances of the language, we tend to be too literal in our spoken English, which comes across as harsh and demanding. For those who never have to master a foreign language—which was most people I met in my early days in America—there is little empathy for this lack of proficiency.

I began to focus on changing the way I spoke. I paid close attention to how senior managers expressed themselves. I learned to adopt the words and phrases they used to achieve the desired results. Instead of bluntly asking "Why?" I learned to use phrases such as "Can you help me understand?" I learned to build on other people's viewpoints by saying, "To your point, let me add that ..."

This is where the American corporate attitudes become very confusing and nuanced. Corporate America likes to promote individualism but it also values teamwork. It was important to show my initiative, but it was also important to show that I was a team player. By listening to and acknowledging others' viewpoints, I built trust and goodwill. This invariably led to better acceptance of my ideas by others.

On the other hand, I learned that I needed to believe in my own ideas and trust my own instincts. They were usually correct. If I had a question, everyone else most likely had the same question. If something didn't seem right, the question needed to be raised to get at the truth. It was important to be true to myself and defend my integrity, even if doing so made me uncomfortable.

My value system was fully formed when I came to America as an adult. There were deep-seated conflicts between my Chinese upbringing and the American corporate values. My timid, self-effacing ways didn't help me. Some of the homespun values and behavior that I was taught in my Chinese youth simply didn't work. It was a huge personal challenge to fundamentally change the way I was taught to interact socially in order to survive and do well in Corporate America.

Hence, the persistent tug-of-war between the two cultures that lasted throughout my professional career. The conflict went beyond the struggle between my insecurities and my ambitions. It went to the core of what I was taught in my youth about what's right and what's wrong. It was a battle between the Chinese values I was taught and the new attitudes I must adapt in order to succeed in my new country. The conflict created a lot of internal stress.

In the end, it was about finding the right balance: how to express my ideas and defend my convictions without assaulting the sensitivity of others; how to be true to myself, be honest and direct, and yet be thoughtful of others' feelings; how to get things done without violating the dignity of others. Finding the right balance continues to be a work-in-progress and a source of personal growth and development for me.

24

From International Subsidiaries to Foreign Joint Ventures

WHEN MOTOROLA UNVEILED the world's first commercial handheld cell phone in 1984, customers lined up in droves to buy the phone. Nicknamed "the brick," the phone weighed two pounds and gave only a half-hour of talk time. It sold for $3,995. Two years later Motorola introduced the Bravo numeric pager. It became the world's best-selling pager. Motorola was quickly becoming a household name for wireless devices around the world.

As Motorola went global, its business operations also changed. To give its global customers a one-stop-shop for all their product needs, Motorola's Communications Sector (referred to as the Comm Sector) formed the International Group in the 1990s. Establishing in-country operations was the new way of doing business in a global market.

My reputation while working as Manager of the Corporate Briefing Room function earned me an invitation by the Financial Controller to join the newly formed International Group. My new job was Manager of Financial Systems. The move from Corporate to Comm Sector was a big promotion and I jumped at it. The fly in the ointment was that my new manager Bob, a crusty old IT (Information Technology) guy, didn't like me for obvious reasons. After all, he didn't hire me. I was forced on him by the user community. In the beginning, the feeling was mutual. Happily, our relationship was saved by Lisa—the Apple Lisa.

Bob had just purchased a $10,000 Apple Lisa for the office. The Apple Lisa was a personal computer designed by Steve Jobs of Apple Computer, Inc. It was the first commercially sold personal computer to have a graphical user interface (GUI), which is the use of graphics and icons instead of English-like keyboard commands. Bob and I were fascinated by the visual capabilities of the new computer with its drag-and-drop operations, pull-down menus, clickable buttons and scroll bars—all driven by a gadget called the mouse. The Apple Lisa was friendly, fun, and easy to use. As Bob and I worked side-by-side to learn to use the Apple Lisa, we found in each other a kindred spirit. Over time, we developed a great rapport and friendship.

The Apple Lisa was far too expensive and thus failed completely in the marketplace. Eventually IBM PCs dominated the market, but Apple would be forever remembered as the innovative company behind the first GUI-based personal computer. Twenty years later, the Apple name with its line of iPods, iPhones, and iPads, would re-emerge on the consumer electronics market with a vengeance, telling the greatest corporate comeback story of all time.

My first assignment in the International Group was to develop a Five-Year Financial Systems Plan for Motorola's international subsidiaries. Sounds daunting? It was. I had to come up with a plan on what we should do with our General Ledger, Payables, and Receivables systems in these foreign countries in the next five years. It was an enormous leap from my Briefing Room responsibilities. I had no idea what a five-year plan looked like, let alone a plan for a business in a foreign country that I had never been to. Where do I start? I was scared out of my mind that I would lose my job.

It seemed obvious, but it took me a while to figure out that I needed to get out of my office to get this done. What are the accounting rules and regulations in the country? How do they affect Motorola? What are Motorola's business plans for the country in the next five years? I couldn't sit in my office and expect the answers to come to me. I could only do so much with a phone call, and there was no email and no Internet at the time.

The only way I could get information was to go there. So I made travel re-
quests to go to the U.K., Australia, Japan, Mexico, Israel, and Canada. I
never got to Israel. The week before I was to depart for Tel Aviv, a terrorist
attack on a tourist bus prompted all company travels to the region to be
halted.

Was it my choice to fly all over the world and face unknown situations
and unfamiliar people? No. I was too timid by nature to seek such adventures. Besides, I was a mother of two young children under the age of ten.
Being gone for two weeks at a time was a real hardship. But I needed to
prove that I could do the job. So I packed my bags, made babysitting arrangements, and traveled thousands of miles to countries I had merely seen
on a map previously. I had no idea what I would do once I got there. I
would figure it out as I went along.

Those were the early days of doing business overseas. Companies had
little experience and few rules regarding international business travels. The
business traveler enjoyed unprecedented perks. Airline travel was business-
class if not first-class. Hotels were five-star. We ate at the finest restaurants.
Everywhere I went I was treated as a VIP. My frequent travels earned me
airline upgrades, express airport security checks, and the use of first-class
airport lounges complete with full buffets and premium alcohol. It was a
whirlwind.

At the Motorola offices, I was surprised by the hospitality and helpful-
ness of the local staff. They cleared their calendars to make time to talk to
me and to answer all my questions. The reason for the cooperation? I was
from Corporate. The report that I would give when I got back to the States
would directly affect how the local operations would be perceived by the
power brokers at headquarters. Such was the nature of corporate politics,
but I was happy to be the lucky benefactor. Through a series of meetings, I
gathered information on local regulations and how accounting practices
could make or break the bottom-line. Like a frog out of the bottom of the
well and seeing the blue sky for the first time, I caught glimpses of the new
globalization process. I saw Motorola in the context of foreign countries
and I was happy to see how much the Motorola brand was respected.
Armed with first-hand knowledge and insights, my report began to take

shape. Nine months later, I completed my assignment and issued the first Motorola International Group Five-year Financial Systems Plan.

The feedback was tremendous. One day, a Motorola executive who was on his way to his new post in Australia came into my office. He asked me for a copy of the five-year plan to better understand the financial reporting requirements in Australia. I felt validated.

Not too long after I joined the Comm Sector's International Group, Bob was replaced by John. John arrived from Phoenix, where he had headed up the computing function for Motorola's Semi-conductors business. He was brought in by the General Manager to create a world-class computing support organization for the International Group.

John set out to reorganize the team. There were six group managers under John. My focus was financial systems and my job was to manage a team of six programmers responsible for the development and maintenance of operations support systems. My team also provided the helpdesk support for a new generation of office equipment—Personal Computers (PCs) that were beginning to show up in many departments. This was my first people management job.

I found that I had a knack for people management. I tried to set a good example by working harder than those who worked for me. I learned to recruit talent, evaluate performance, mentor subordinates, and manage a budget.

My team fondly called me the "dragon lady." There were two reasons for the nickname: I had a "do or die" attitude about deadlines and commitments, and I never backed away from tough decisions, such as firing someone who didn't perform. However, I was also supportive and appreciative. I made it a point to recognize and reward good performance by being generous with promotions and pay raises. Special monetary awards were handed out for good teamwork and extra effort. I found the mentoring and career development aspects of my job especially rewarding.

During this time, Motorola instituted a bonus program to encourage employees to make cost-saving and profit-improvement suggestions. The program was called Participative Management Program (PMP). Even though I was a cynic when it came to this sort of company programs, I was competitive and I liked to win. So I entered the competition with my team and led them to win first place within the International Group. We won with a project called "Easy Money" aimed at improving Motorola's accounts receivables. For our win, the entire team was sent to Disney World in Orlando Florida as the reward.

My new manager John and I got along very well from the start. When John got a promotion to transfer to a new business unit called the International Networks Division (IND), he asked me to join him. The business unit would be headed by Janiece, my friend and mentor whom I met a couple of years ago on the plane to Australia.

In the mid-1990s, Motorola's paging business was booming. Having introduced the Bravo numeric pager a decade ago, Motorola now launched its second-generation product, the two-way pager. The Tango two-way personal messaging pager allowed users to receive text messages and reply with canned responses. This had the potential for applications that users never dreamed of. All of a sudden, it was possible to contact anyone on the go and get a response back. The low cost of pagers and paging services meant that everyday people could afford to own a pager. Overnight, the use of pagers exploded. Every doctor, sales rep, manager, real estate agent, and utility worker in the U.S. was carrying a pager. It was time to get an even bigger piece of the pie. It was time to educate folks around the world on the usefulness of this wireless technology.

As Motorola launched the global campaign to promote the utility of wireless communications, two new divisions were formed to advance the sale of cell phones and pagers respectively. The International Networks Division (IND) that I joined was focused on bringing paging to third world countries. To do so Motorola would establish Joint Ventures with local businesses. The business model was for Motorola to provide the capital, the know-how, and the training. In return, we got a foot in the door. In most cases, we were allowed to own no more than 49 percent of the business, but it was a means to an end.

It was an exciting time. We were at the dawn of a new era. Wireless was poised to forever change the way people live and communicate. During the four years that I worked in IND, Motorola launched paging and wireless data joint venture businesses in Frankfurt Germany, Bangalore India,

Sao Paulo Brazil, Moscow Russia, Jakarta Indonesia, Tokyo Japan, and the former British colony of Hong Kong. I traveled to all of these countries.

My job at IND was to set up the IT infrastructure to ensure the smooth daily operations of the Joint Venture business. My duties included the recruitment and hiring of local IT managers, overseeing the installation of the back-office support systems, and contracting secured and reliable telecommunications connections for the business. I also helped launch call centers for the paging business. It was exciting to be part of something so big and revolutionary.

The travel was grueling. Oftentimes, I woke up in hotel rooms wondering where I was and what time zone I was in. The five-star hotels and expense-paid restaurant meals made business travel look glamorous, but behind the scenes, it was incredibly hard work. On top of the jet lag and the time changes, I had to be mentally on all the time. Being in a foreign country meant that I had to deal with unforeseen issues and circumstances, so I had to be constantly thinking on my feet. And the business travels were not all fun and glitz either. There were regular delays in airports, long layovers, lost luggage, and over-booked hotels, all of which added to the misery of the world traveler.

But I did enjoy seeing the world and learning about the countries that I never thought I would have the chance to visit. On occasions when I traveled to the Asia region, I took advantage of the added benefit of being able to hop over to Macau to see my parents.

Professionally it was a period of tremendous personal growth. Having to deal with people and problems in a foreign country added a layer of complexity to my job. There were cultural issues, language issues, and technology issues. The most eye-opening experience for me was learning how work habits and attitudes differed so much in each country. I learned to appreciate those differences and leverage them to get the job done. I made the following observations:

- The Germans were disciplined and had a great respect for rules and structure. They tended however to be rigid and inflexible. It was an exercise in futility to disagree with a German. They were almost always right. In any case, you would never get them to change their minds unless you could produce written rules and procedures to the contrary.

- The Japanese were respectful and courteous. They adhered to strict protocols based on seniority and rank. They didn't like to disagree in public. However, you couldn't take their politeness as concurrence. They would nod and gesture in agreement, but turn around and do something completely different than what you thought had been agreed to at the meeting. The Japanese valued relationships and business courtesy. It worked best if you could get them to agree in private discussions before the official meetings took place.

- The Mexicans were friendly and cooperative. Titles were important to them. Everyone was a manager. To get work done you needed to find the real worker-bees. Those tended to be the handful of women at the bottom of an inverted pyramid organizational structure, with lots of male managers at the top, as the culture was still chauvinistic. However, the stereotypical "mañana" attitude was changing, with modern managers taking on a greater sense of urgency in order to be competitive in the global market.

- The Indians were smart and driven. They were resourceful and resilient people. When we were working in India in the mid-1990s, the power would go out on a daily basis, and sometimes even hourly. In the middle of a meeting, the power would go out and someone would unflappably go down to the basement, crank up the generator, and come right back to resume the discussions as if nothing had happened. The country was very poor. There was a quiet desperation to get ahead. When we posted two job openings in Bangalore, we got over five thousand applicants. Special trucks had to be hired to bring in the applications.

Equally important were the social interactions. Drinking beer with the Germans, singing karaoke with the Japanese, and joining in a game of bowling with the Mexicans broke down barriers—cultural, social, and language barriers—and the barriers between "us" and "them," "them" meaning the people sent from Corporate to spy on the locals.

My International Joint Ventures escapade was an enthralling and enriching experience, one that would change my perspectives forever. I attribute my success during this part of my career to two things: my empathy for local differences as a foreigner myself, and John's mentorship.

Between the International Group and IND, John and I worked together for over eight years. During this time, we traveled the globe together. We shared the love of travel. We both enjoyed learning foreign cultures, history and traditions, meeting people with different ways of thinking, and indulging in the diversity of local cuisines. Even though we both had strong opinions, we learned to negotiate our differences. I learned a great deal from John's experience and his macro big-picture way of thinking. In return, John valued my analytical ability and my keen intuition. We made a great team. John was responsible for my highest promotion within Motorola—that of Director of Business Systems.

My experience working for John was a counter-point to my many negative experiences with other male managers. In my career, John stood out as the shining example of good corporate management. Gender didn't matter; it was the individual who made the difference. Men and women who value fairness, who are open-minded to look for the best in all people, who are strong in their convictions and their actions—they are the kind of managers that make Corporate America great.

Ironically, talking about what makes Corporate America great reminds me of a shocking management style that set a disgraceful trend around the time I worked in IND. Gender had nothing to do with this trend.

During the late 1980s and early 1990s, a corporate culture of management by intimidation brewed within Corporate America and made its way into Motorola. To be fair, it was the culture revered by many CEOs during that period. This was the "Donald Trump" style of management by fear: "If you don't do it, I'll find someone else who will." It was widely accepted and considered a very effective management style. Upper management used fear and intimidation to get results. Successful management was supposed to be impersonal, hard driving, and measured by the numbers, often leaving a trail of bodies in its path.

As a member of the senior support staff, I routinely attended operations reviews—meetings where the performance of a business operation was critiqued. There I witnessed how management by intimidation was carried out. In a brightly lit conference room, the senior staff sat around the large mahogany conference table. The support staff sat on chairs lined up against the wall in case we were called on to answer specific questions. Two empty chairs at the end of the table were reserved for the General Manager and his Controller.

His Eminence would always be the last person to enter the room. It would start with him making some small joke and everyone feeling obliged to laugh. Then the room quieted as his piercing eyes scanned the nervous faces, looking for the first victim.

When the target victim had been identified, the browbeating began.

"What do you mean we are not going to make these numbers? Who owns these numbers? Who? I want to know who is accountable!"

"That was the stupidest decision! Who made the call? Did *you* make the call?"

"Everyone get out of the room except *you*!"

"Anyone who disagrees with what I just said, there is the door."

"I want *you* to resign now. Give me your badge."

"I'm convinced *you* cannot make that forecast. Barry, do you have your checkbook? I'll bet you five hundred dollars that Tom *won't* make the forecast. What do you say?"

Oftentimes the drama was created for theatrical effect only. The threats and firings seldom, if at all, got carried out. But the verbal abuse was personal. The in-your-face reprimands were degrading. Respect for personal dignity went out of the window. Upper management thought it was effective to inflict pain, discomfort, and anger in people in order to drive results.

For those who were sensitive or thin-skinned, this was a brutal era. The intimidation tactics were pervasive across the corporation. I could dodge the bullets in my own department because of John acting as our intermediary, but I couldn't avoid the bullying behavior in the customer departments that I served. I learned that I couldn't take things too personally. I tried to convince myself that the person acting out these theatrics didn't really mean it, that they were actually wonderful husbands and fathers at home and that this was only done for show. But it was a gut wrenching experience to see such bullying in action.

I was not proud of the way I had to survive during these brutal times. It was not in my nature to be confrontational, but when I was faced with bullying behavior, it took all my strength not to let go with my anger and hit back. Yet I had to consider the consequences. I couldn't risk my job. I couldn't afford to burn any bridges. So instead, I wrote screaming emails that went into my garbage can. I lowered my voice and resorted to my demure Chinese demeanor to avoid the fight. I had to remind myself, "This will go away if I just ignore them. If I can just hang on, things will change for the better." Eventually this management style did pass. I stayed around Motorola long enough to see the return of rational leadership. In looking back, I don't know if I had any choice in my silence. I didn't like the way I had to stifle my feelings and swallow my pride, but I'm glad I survived to see future chapters of my career being written.

About four years into my IND job, things in the communications world changed again. The wireless business was beginning to mature. There was no longer the need to operate Joint Ventures in country in order to promote the use of pagers and cell phones. Wireless operators around the world were becoming well entrenched, and they were our customers. As manufacturers, our goal was to avoid running businesses that would compete with our customers. It was time to exit the Joint Venture business.

One day, the entire IND department was called into a large conference room. Many more stationed around the world were on the conference line. The General Manager announced that IND had been dissolved and everyone in the division had officially lost their jobs. We were given a limited amount of time to look for another job within Motorola. I found myself in a desperate position scrambling to find another position before the clock ran out.

25

An Accidental Engineer

IF SOMEONE HAD told me I would spend over ten years in a top engineering job, I would have laughed in his or her face. There was not an engineering bone in my body. I was good at the soft stuff—planning, communicating, analyzing, strategizing—those were my forte. In no way was I mechanically, mathematically, or scientifically inclined. A job that dealt with technology, radio sciences, and engineering principles couldn't have been farther away from my career aspirations.

When it was announced that the entire Joint Ventures business operation would be shut down and that I had to find another job, it came at a very bad time. I was a single mother supporting two teen-age children. Ryan was just entering college. With my seniority and my compensation, I knew my best bet was to stay with Motorola rather than starting over with another company. I called everyone I knew and applied to every position that opened up. It was at a time of multiple waves of downsizing, so openings were few and competition was fierce. But I managed to find three options.

The first was to work for the Chief Marketing Office, a department that had just been created to address marketing and brand development needs, which had long been neglected in Motorola. The second was business development for 4G, a futuristic look at the market opportunities for fourth-generation cellular phones, like—why would anyone want to buy a phone with a camera in it? The third was to direct the Standards Strategy for a new corporate initiative called *Five Nines*.

Okay, you have no idea what I just said. I didn't either. What is Five Nines and what are Standards? When you don't even understand the job title, it is pretty intimidating to consider taking the job. It's like being offered the job of Ombudsman for the University of Timbuktu and you don't know what "Ombudsman" means and where Timbuktu is.

So why did I decide to take the Standards position? The answer was simple. The Five Nines Standards Director job offered the best guarantee for job security. I had a mortgage to pay, food to put on the table, and college tuition to pay for my two children. There would be no gambling with my next assignment. My next job had to be rock solid, or at least one that offered the most stability. So against every nerve in my body, I accepted the job that I least wanted. I became the Director of Standards for Five Nines.

What is Five Nines? It is a quality initiative. Quality has long been a hallmark of Motorola's products. Motorola invented Six Sigma, which became synonymous with the word Quality. The company was a winner of the first annual Malcolm Baldrige National Quality Award. However, Five Nines is not Six Sigma. The goal of Five Nines is to achieve 99.999% system availability and the initiative is to implement the tools to achieve this goal.

Never mind what the term "availability" means and how it is measured. Let's just say that it is highly technical and is tied to quality methodologies to ensure that cellular network failures that cause "blackouts" are kept to an absolute minimum.

Any way you look at it, this was a hard-core engineering job and not a fit for my skills or my disposition. I had no schooling in electrical engineering or standards, no background in quality principles and metrics, and no experience in working in an external-facing job. The folks that I was going to deal with on this assignment would be the brightest and the best in electrical and software engineering, most with the letters Ph.D. after their names.

In spite of the paralyzing fear that loomed over my head, I accepted the job and moved to a large window office in Motorola's Corporate

Tower. Overnight, my world changed from International Joint Ventures to Government Relations and Patent Law.

Why do companies care about standards? An industry standard is a set of specifications that has been approved by an industry body and adopted by the industry as the blueprint for creating a specific product or service. For example, in the automotive industry, there is a standard for tire sizes so that a consumer can purchase a tire from any company and the tire will fit the car made by any auto manufacturer.

Companies do things to make money. Participating in standards comes with the promise of getting patent revenue and having the early-to-market advantage. A lot of money and resources go into new research. If a company's inventions get into the standard, other companies making the product will have to pay the inventing entity royalties for using its technology. So companies with competing technologies battle to get their inventions into the standard.

As a senior level person coming into the job, I was expected to hit the ground running. There was no time to ask dumb questions and no one to whom I could ask those questions. If I couldn't prove that I could do the job, there would be plenty of people lined up at the door to take my job.

How do you prepare for a job so foreign when you have no coach or mentor? The answer came from a surprising new place: the Internet. This was 1998, and the Internet had just debuted. I quickly recognized that the Internet was a tremendous resource. The World Wide Web (www) offered for the first time a powerful encyclopedia in the sky and at my fingertips. Almost any topic was searchable. The wealth of information was astounding even in those early days of first-generation search engines. For the first six months of my new job, I spent the days running searches and the evenings reading everything I had downloaded during the day. I found enough information to fill a six-drawer cabinet in my office. I felt like I was taking an advanced self-study degree program on standards. It was one of the toughest courses I had ever taken, especially since I didn't have an instructor or a program guide.

As if cramming for a difficult exam, I willed myself to learn all about the international standards landscape and to sort through the alphabet soup of telecommunications standards organizations such as the ITU, the TIA, the CTIA, the IETF, and the IEEE.

Because standards are international, my job came with a heavy requirement for international travels. Before I could catch my breath, I was on a plane to Cork, Ireland to attend my first standards meeting.

It was the spring of 1998. I flew to Heathrow Airport and connected on an Aer Lingus flight to Ireland to attend the meeting of the industry standards group called the 3GPP (3rd Generation Partnership Program), which was tasked with the creation of technical specifications for a 3G (3rd Generation) cellular communications system.

At the time of this writing, the world is no longer a stranger to 3G services on their cell phones, but in 1998, the brightest of engineering minds were hard at work to make 3G happen. Simply put, the objective of 3rd generation wireless was to provide wireless services anytime anywhere, and to support not just telephone voice calls but text and video at higher speeds. It would take another four years before Motorola would launch its first 3G nationwide network in 2002.

The meeting was held in a medium-sized conference room in a Motorola facility. Companies took turns hosting the meetings, and Motorola Ireland happened to be the meeting host. This particular working group dealt with a technical topic called the Network Management standards—standards for managing cellular infrastructure equipment such as base stations. There were approximately fifty people in attendance from ten-plus companies. The room was packed.

The tone of the meeting was formal. The committee chair and vice-chair presided over the proceedings. There was also a secretary to record meeting minutes. The chair called the meeting to order and began reading the rules and regulations governing the meeting conduct. Everyone in the room was expected to have reviewed the documents contributed by the participating companies and universities. Then the action began.

Word by word the specifications were dissected, debated, and voted on. Those who wanted to make comments for or against the proposals must follow the right protocol, which in most cases stuck to Robert's Rules. The discussions were often spirited, depending on the personalities involved. Because the participants' job was to defend their company's positions, and because those positions were often in conflict with each other, reaching consensus was a herculean task and at times downright confrontational.

I was lost. I had not read any of the documents. Worse yet, I couldn't figure out how to connect to the on-site wireless network to access the document server. I looked around the room and saw a sea of foreign faces, mostly male. I craned my head to try to keep up with the discussions. They were speaking a language I didn't understand—the language of technology and standards.

The standards world had a sizable vocabulary of its own. It was chock-full of acronyms. Furthermore, the concepts being debated were way over my head. As standards deal with future innovations in technology, the participants were discussing very advanced concepts in radio sciences and telecommunications hardware and software. To participate in the discussions you must have a solid knowledge of the underlying technology. I was a fish out of water.

There was another language issue. Because standards are global, standards participants come from every part of the world. English was the spoken language in the meetings, but that didn't mean that everyone spoke English the same way. The Irish, Italian, and Danish attendees spoke so differently from the German and the French. English spoken by Mainland Chinese, Korean, and Japanese attendees sounded like Mandarin, Korean, and Japanese, as the speaker tended to intonate the same way they did in their mother tongue. There was hardly anything that I could recognize as American English. All I heard were singsong voices, throaty expressions, and indiscernible enunciations that bore no resemblance to the spoken English I knew.

It was déjà vu. I was back in 1969, newly arrived in a foreign country without speaking the language or understanding the accents.

Mercifully, the morning coffee break came none too soon. Relieved, I made my way to the refreshment area where small groups had gathered. I mustered my courage and nonchalantly walked up to one of the groups. A roar of laughter broke out and I leaned in to listen. The topic of hilarity was Viagra. The Food and Drug Administration (FDA) had just approved the use of the drug Viagra to treat male impotence. Everyone had a joke on the topic. I felt awkward, as I was the only female in the room. My instinct was to turn on my heels, but I made myself stay. I knew that I must learn to find my footing in the testosterone-charged crowd if I wanted to stay in standards.

The standards populace was over 90% male. If women engineers were considered geeks, women engineers who worked in standards were viewed as super-nerds. Most female standards participants came from Asia with a minority from Europe. A handful of them were whip smart and assertive. Most, however, stayed in the background. Socially they tended to keep to co-workers from their home company. If I was looking for camaraderie and friendship, I was in the wrong place.

I quickly learned that the process of making standards was arduous and intense. Face-to-face meetings, like the one I was attending, were scheduled every other month, but the real work actually took place between meetings and went on year-round at a crushing pace through teleconferences and email exchanges.

To a right-brained person like me, the standards work was dry, the meetings long, and the discussions tedious. But failing in my job was not an option, nor did I want to just get by. I made it my mission to find my niche. Happily, I discovered that I was a quick study and I was able to make sense of very technical material. I was surprised to find that my ability to zero in on the issues and my obsessive attitude towards problem solving applied well to standards. My lack of technical background actually allowed me to pull myself away from the details, connect the dots, and see the big picture of how the standard would impact Motorola.

Instead of being buried in the minutia of document editing, I focused on the business issues and quickly learned what I needed to do to influence the standard to Motorola's advantage. I took every opportunity to gather intelligence on the technology developments in other companies. I networked feverishly, focusing on building relationships to lay the groundwork for strategic company-to-company partnerships. I was amazed how quickly I began to negotiate the nuances of strategy making. On the technology front, I was determined to build my subject matter expertise. Google became my best friend and teacher. I found that I had a knack for deciphering difficult concepts and explaining them to others in simple, easy-to-understand terms. In spite of my lack of academic background, I became the spokesperson on very technical matters. One year after I started in standards, I gave a talk on *Web-based Network Management for IP Networks* to an audience of over two hundred in a conference in Nice, France.

I was an accidental engineer. Out of the necessity to hold down a well-paying job so that I could provide for my family, I reinvented myself. With unyielding determination, I squeezed my Bachelor-of-Arts brain into a Doctor-of-Philosophy persona. It was an unexpected and incredible journey. Along the way, I met hugely talented and uncommonly interesting people from the mightiest corporations and the biggest universities around the world. These encounters humbled, inspired and enriched me.

26

China and I

I HAVE ALWAYS dreaded the question "Where are you from?" I've never been sure if I should say I am an American, a Chinese, a Chinese-American, or a Chicagoan. When I first came to America, I told people I was from Macau. They didn't know where Macau was and they were not looking for geography in my answer. After I was naturalized, I answered that I was American. That wasn't the answer they were looking for either. I have an Asian face. They wanted to know if I was Chinese, Korean, Japanese, or something else.

When I first traveled to China, I was surprised when the locals asked if I was Korean or Japanese. Something in my appearance told them that I wasn't native. Again the dilemma: Should I tell them that I am an American or should I make sure that they know that I'm a full-blooded Chinese?

Ironically, in my youth, I wasn't proud of being Chinese. People from colonies like Hong Kong and Macau had no allegiance to any sovereignty. I came from the generation of Hong Kong and Macau people who couldn't wait to leave for economic reasons. When I arrived in America, discrimination against Chinese had waned, but people of color, including Asians, were still looked down on. It was only until recent years when China rose to prominence in economic status that we saw a rise in Chinese patriotism and Chinese pride. So by the time I set foot on mainland Chinese soil for the first time in my life, everything I had learned about China in my youth had been turned upside down. I was confused and conflicted.

What brought me to China? In the early 2000s, China was the awakening giant learning to find its roar. In the world of wireless technology, the object of envy was Intellectual Property (IP). IP is the patented knowledge for a particular technology. Having paid millions of dollars in royalties to American and European companies to develop their telecommunications industry, China was determined to build up its own IP arsenal. It looked to IP-rich partners such as Motorola and Ericsson to kick-start its own research and development efforts.

One of my assignments during this period was to work on next-generation cell phone technology coined "Beyond 3G." The goal of Beyond-3G was to offer better than 3G multimedia services on the cell phone.

Motorola had a long and successful history in China, having opened its first office in Beijing in 1987. In 1992, Motorola (China) Electronics Ltd. was formed and a manufacturing facility was set up in the city of Tianjin to produce pagers, semiconductors, two-way radios, automobile electronics, and later mobile phones. Motorola entered into partnerships with many local Chinese companies and enjoyed a great relationship with the Chinese government. The Motorola brand was well respected in China, and in the early 2000s, Motorola was regarded as the most successful foreign company in China.

It was during these golden years of Motorola-China partnership that I traveled to Beijing to work with China's most prestigious research universities, including institutions such as Beijing University of Posts and Telecommunications (BUPT) and Tsinghua University.

During these trips, I saw a China bursting with excitement and anticipation. It was a country anxiously waiting its turn on the world stage. The students and professors I met were bright and eager to engage. Many research institutes were on the verge of changing their business model from just being learning institutions to self-funding profit-seeking entities. It was the dawn of a new way of thinking. For a long time China had been fighting its tainted image of selling fake and counterfeit goods in violation of other countries' Intellectual Property Rights (IPR) and Trademarks. Now poised to develop its own IP stockpile, China was anxious to learn about the protection of IP Rights.

When I traveled to Beijing, I took on the role of subject matter expert representing Motorola, often giving talks in symposiums and workshops on the topic of Intellectual Property Rights and protection of those rights. When the U.S. Trade Representative (USTR) office hosted a *China-U.S. Standards and Conformity Assessment Workshop* in Beijing in August of 2004, I was invited to give a talk on "IPR *Policy as an Enabler in Effective Standardization.*"

On these occasions, I came to Beijing with mixed emotions. I was proud to be a Motorola spokesperson and to be treated like a VIP, but I felt like a stranger in the country of my ancestry. I was embarrassed that I couldn't speak Mandarin. I felt once again the sting of being an outsider. Again, it raised the questions, *Who am I? Where do I belong?*

These questions would continue to haunt me. Am I more American or am I more Chinese? In my forty-plus years in America, I have become completely Americanized. I cling closely to my American identity. I dress American, talk American, and carry myself in American ways. I am what they would call a *Banana* or a *Twinkie*—yellow on the outside but white on the inside. I relate to American norms and values much more than I do Chinese ones. But when I am in China, I feel an intimate connection with the Chinese people, and I have an affectionate understanding of what it is to be Chinese.

In a way, I am glad that my children will be spared the same conundrum. They are Americans with Chinese blood. Against America's multicultural backdrop, there is hardly any confusion at all. They both married white. Their children will not have any strong hints of Chinese in their appearance. I hope, however, that they will always know that they are part Chinese and be proud of that part of their heritage. When I look into the future, I see a true global village, where everyone comes from somewhere, but no one is defined by where they come from.

27

A Seat on the IEEE Standards Board

IN 2005, MOTOROLA made a comeback as a market leader with the Motorola RAZR line. It sold over 120 million units reclaiming its number two position in the field of mobile phone manufacturers. To ensure continued success, the company accelerated its focus on not just top-line growth but bottom-line profit. Cost cutting became an increasingly important tool. Raising Motorola's profile in industry standards in order to reinforce its leadership image also became an important initiative. It was at this time that my career would take another huge unexpected turn.

A new department manager, Mario, was hired from Florida to replace the manager who retired. Mario came from the operations side with a reputation for driving up performance and driving down costs. He was a pragmatic manager who saw a department of high-grade, highly paid individuals, and immediately set out to "trim the fat." He dismissed one-third of the staff immediately. It was an unnerving time because we all felt that we were under close scrutiny, and that anyone could be the next to go.

I was working on next-generation public safety standards, primarily with a new standards consortium called Project Mesa, a European initiative. Its goal was to tackle the standards for the next-generation communications systems for first responders, such as police and firefighters, and for disaster relief in the event of earthquakes, hurricanes, terrorist attacks, and other catastrophic events. The consortium, however, was poorly organized and the progress was slow.

One day I was called into Mario's office.

"It has come to my attention that a board seat has just opened up at the IEEE Standards Board. It would be good for Motorola to get that seat. I want you to make a run for it."

The IEEE is the premier standards organization that gave us the revolutionary Wi-Fi standard—the standard that became synonymous with wireless. Because of the Wi-Fi standard, we are able to access the internet anywhere we go. The IEEE, or Institute of Electrical and Electronics Engineers, was founded over a hundred years ago, and is the world's largest organization for engineering professionals.

The IEEE-Standards Association (IEEE-SA) Standards Board is the oversight committee for IEEE standards. The companies who sit on the board include some of the biggest names in their industries. The people representing these companies on the IEEE board are senior level managers overseeing standards in their companies.

It was obvious that Mario felt that I was under-utilized and under-challenged. He was pushing me to do more. But I couldn't believe what he had asked me to do.

Like the Incredible Hulk under extreme stress, my insecurities came raging out. I was convinced that I had no qualifications for such a job. I had no experience serving on any board, let alone a powerful industry board. I was an unknown within the IEEE circles. I had no impressive academic or industry credentials. I had no idea what a standards board member was expected to do. Even if I were nominated because of Motorola's clout, I would fail miserably on the job. The only recourse I had was to quit. I seriously considered the option.

The soul searching began. Am I ready to quit? Have I ever run away from something because I was scared? Am I ready to walk out of a job that I have fought hard to keep for twenty-five years? Will I look back and regret such a decision? After many sleepless nights, I decided that I wanted to stay on at Motorola. I told Mario that I would welcome the opportunity. The following week, Mario submitted my nomination with a formal letter detailing Motorola's support and sponsorship.

Secretly I was hoping that the IEEE-SA would decline my nomination, but it was not to be. In December of 2004, I received a letter from the IEEE-SA Standards Board (SASB) chair welcoming me to the board and to the first board meeting in the upcoming year.

In the spring of 2005, I took the first of many flights to the IEEE headquarters in Piscataway New Jersey—a quiet college town (Rutgers University) and bedroom community about thirty-five miles outside of New York City. There were four board meetings a year, with three of them being held at the IEEE headquarters. I met my fellow board members, most of them from big-name companies such as Intel, HP, IBM, Lucent, and Siemens. I was the only woman on the twenty-five-seat board. At my first meeting, I was warmly received by the IEEE-SA staff, who greeted me with, "It's so good to see a woman on the standards board."

The board meeting was held in the large conference room in the walk-out basement of the IEEE building. The set-up was formal. Tables were arranged in two rows of concentric semi-circles covered with white table-cloths. Board members sat in the first row with assigned seats marked by nameplates. A shiny microphone for each board member was planted right next to his nameplate. Non-voting members sat in the second row. Guests and the IEEE-SA support staff sat on one side of the room with chairs arranged five rows deep. It made me think of the United Nations.

The chair presided over the meeting flanked by the past chair and the chair-in-waiting. An IEEE lawyer was in attendance to address any legal issues that might come up during the meeting.

The chair called the meeting to order followed by a round of introductions by everyone present. When my turn came, I was ready with my calm and confident act. As I spoke, I made eye contact with everyone around the room. When I announced my name and my affiliation with Motorola, a surge of pride swelled in me. I was the representative of a company that was well respected among its peers. I felt a sense of legitimacy.

As an oversight organization, the IEEE-SA not only oversaw the development and revision of IEEE standards but also the governance aspects of due process, openness, and fairness. The topics that came before the Board ranged from how to deal with the abuse of dominance in the working group to whether intellectual properties contributed to standards should be royalty-free.

The meeting was uneventful. Approvals were granted almost as a matter of routine. The heavy-duty work behind the consent agenda had already been done in subcommittees prior to the board meeting. A string of somewhat boring committee reports, legal updates, and procedural discussions followed. They were saved by interjections of topics that required serious deliberations. I quickly grasped the parliamentary process, and to my own surprise, I had no difficulty raising my hand and jumping into the debates. My peers were supportive. They actually listened to what I had to say. I found some of the more controversial subjects fascinating and thought provoking, particularly when they collided with my personal beliefs. On those issues, I had no problem finding my voice and speaking up. The meeting lasted from 8:30 a.m. to 3:30 p.m. By 6:00 p.m., I was on my flight back to Chicago.

I had survived my first board meeting. Over time, I gained confidence, and the constant pinch of panic in my stomach gradually went away. I actually began to take pleasure in the role I was playing on the Standards Board. My contributions earned the respect of my fellow board members. I was invited to serve for a full three-year term.

During my term on the board, I campaigned tirelessly for Motorola to win the IEEE-SA Corporate Standards Award and succeeded in bringing home the glass-globe trophy in 2006. The award was given for outstanding leadership and contribution to the IEEE standards. Motorola could now be counted among such companies as Intel, Lucent, Sony, and IBM, all of which were past recipients of the award.

The period from 2005 to 2007 was a tumultuous period for the IEEE-SA. The controversy was centered on whether powerful companies were using their money and their clout to game the IEEE standards-making process. In 2006, a bitter dispute broke out between two leading wireless mobile standards. The dispute involved four very high profile companies. It was alleged that one of the companies had hired paid consultants and used monopolistic tactics to stack the vote in their favor. The Standards Board had the task of deciding whether abuse had occurred, and if it had, the fate of the standards working group.

These deliberations were held in closed sessions, and the board members were not given prior notice. At the first of these meetings, I sat and listened to the decision that the Standards Board was tasked to make. In an instant, I was struck with the realization that I had a conflict of interest: The Company I was working for had a stake in the outcome of the IEEE Standards Board's decision. My sense of fairness told me that I couldn't be part of the decision-making process.

I raised my hand and asked to address the chair. I explained that I couldn't be a participant in deciding the outcome because the company I worked for had a material interest in the outcome. I asked to be excused from the proceedings on the grounds of conflict of interest.

The legal counsel representing the Standards Board was present at the meeting. She applauded me for my actions. The rest of the board was then polled for their conflict of interest. Those who declared that they were conflicted were excused from the deliberations. Following the meeting, the Board adopted new rules to recuse board members who were "conflicted" on specific board decisions.

When I reflect on what happened that day, I am surprised at how quickly I came to the decision and how instinctively I acted. In speaking up, I had taken a huge risk. I had broken a self-imposed rule of not making waves, of not calling attention to myself. What if others thought my action was unfounded? What if they thought I was a troublemaker to raise an issue on something that up until then had not been perceived as a problem? I would have been thoroughly embarrassed in front of my peers. But I am proud to have taken the risk. I realize that every time I am able to step out of my comfort zone to do what I think is right, I feel empowered.

28

Becoming Chair of SCC41

HAVE YOU EVER wondered what is the full extent of your potential? Do you know what you're really capable of? Have you ever been pushed to the limit and lived through it to discover your own greatness? Most of us are never given the opportunity. I am one of the lucky few who had the chance to experience this.

In the mid-2000s, more and more people were using email, text messaging, video chat, and other social media, driving up the demand for greater bandwidth and higher Internet speeds. The corporate research team in Motorola was starting to work on a new technology called Cognitive Radio and Dynamic Spectrum Access Networks (DYSPAN), which would dramatically improve the speed and quality of information for mobile users. A newly proposed standards group called SCC41 was designed to create a whole family of standards around this new technology.

In 2007, I was happily serving on the IEEE Standards Board for the third term. I was now a seasoned board member. I knew my way around the organization and how to get things done. I had earned the respect of my fellow board members. I was mentally prepared for the June 2007 board meeting to be business as usual.

During the meeting, however, the board went into a closed session to deal with a personnel issue. The issue had to do with the leadership in SCC41. The controversy centered on the question of whether the organizer of the standard, Burke, should be appointed the chair of the standard due to certain conflicts. While sitting in the meeting, I was distracted by a text message from American Airlines that bad weather had caused my flight back to Chicago to be cancelled and that I had been booked on a flight for the next day. I was leaving for an Alaskan Cruise the following day so the flight cancellation created a problematic situation for me. Determined not to miss my cruise, I excused myself from the meeting to make other flight arrangements. When I returned to the meeting room, to my surprise I was greeted by congratulations from my colleagues. The chair had appointed me co-chair of SCC41, and the Board had unanimously voted its approval.

So what was the problem? Motorola wanted me to take the prestigious position, but I was shell-shocked. The job of chair for a Standards Coordinating Committee (SCC) is similar to that of running a nonprofit start-up company except with the roles of CEO, COO, and CTO combined. The chair had to define the vision, the strategic goals, and the business plan. The chair also had to run the day-to-day operation of the committee and make sure it was financially solvent. The chair was expected to be a technology guru who could knowledgably steer the direction of the standard.

There were many other challenges for SCC41. The standard lacked in-dustry support because the subject matter was considered by many as aca-demic and blue-sky. The Federal Communications Commission (FCC) reg-ulations that would have given it the necessary impetus had been stalled. The membership was dwindling.

I knew I could deal with the business aspects of running the organiza-tion, but there wouldn't be enough hours in the day for me to get up to speed on the complex technology of dynamic spectrum access. I found comfort in the fact that my co-chair Burke would compensate for my lack of critical expertise. If I make the partnership work, I might be able to pull this off.

I reached out to my co-chair Burke. I wasn't sure if there would be feelings of animosity, but I detected none. Burke was amicable. We worked out how we would collaborate as co-chairs. We would take turns and alter-nate responsibilities. The first SCC41 plenary meeting was scheduled to be held in Berlin, Germany in four months. We agreed that Burke would chair that first meeting.

On December 3, 2007, I walked into the meeting room of the Alcatel-Lucent building in the city of Berlin. By 8:30 a.m., everyone was seated, waiting for the proceedings to begin. My anxiety was building when at 9:00 a.m. Burke still had not shown up. The meeting was half an hour late in opening, and I could no longer stall. It felt almost like an out-of-body experience when I stepped up to the podium completely unprepared for what I was going to say next. I stared into the audience and realized that all eyes were on me. I took a deep breath. As I uttered words of welcome, my voice echoed back to the front of the room. I took a long pause, met the gaze of the audience around the room, and summoning a steady voice, I called the meeting to order. I was winging it, all the while calming myself so that nobody would know how nervous I was. Burke finally arrived an hour later. I chaired the entire four-day meeting by myself.

After the Berlin meeting, Burke resigned. The reason he gave was that he didn't have the sponsorship and funding support to continue in the co-chair role. I became the sole chair of SCC41.

It happened so unexpectedly that I had no time to confront my fears. It was baptism by fire. I rolled up my sleeves and just did it. First, I had to rebuild the leadership team. Then I set out to create structure for our standards work by installing operating procedures. To energize the work program, I issued an open call for new work initiatives. To ensure that SCC41 would attract the best minds, I reached out to universities and research entities to initiate collaborative efforts. Since the technology had applications in military and defense, I also learned to work with government agencies such as the Department of Defense (DOD) and Department of Homeland Security (DHS).

I supervised the standards process, mentored working group chairs, and liaised with industry organizations. I learned to fundraise, organize international events, and manage public relations for SCC41, all on the job. When I was not the boss, I was the floor sweeper, the bottle washer, and whatever else needed to be done.

The stress of the job was all consuming. I lay awake at night worrying about how to grow the membership and invigorate the work in SCC41. The success and failure of the organization weighed heavily on my shoulders. The pressure affected my health. I had problems sleeping and my blood pressure climbed sky high. The combination of a bad prescription and a careless doctor sent me to the hospital twice. A couple of months later I got shingles. Intense pain shot up and down my back. On the opening day of the plenary meetings held in Washington DC, I couldn't get out of bed because of the debilitating pain.

But I pushed through the pain and stoically marched forward. The ironic thing was I really didn't have to answer to anyone but myself in my job as SCC41 chair. Motorola was happy as long as I kept the position. Yet my personal pride and sense of responsibility compelled me to take the job extremely seriously. I worked harder than if my livelihood depended on it.

During my two-year tenure as chair of SCC41, the organization grew and thrived in spite of extremely difficult financial times. It was a challenging environment in which to chair an organization entirely dependent on volunteerism. I saw the development and ratification of three industry standards and installed two new projects into the committee. I earned the hearts, minds, and respect of the membership. When I had to step down from the position two years later due to a change of priorities within Motorola, I was deeply touched by the letters of admiration and appreciation that poured in.

Once in a lifetime an opportunity comes along that demands more of you than you think you're capable of giving. Becoming the chair of SCC41 was such an opportunity. It almost broke me. But I found the strength to stretch myself to the limits of my ability to realize the kind of professional and personal growth that I had never thought was possible for me to attain. I saw my potential and I reached for it.

29

Digital TV, Surveillance Cameras, and Cloud Computing

CHAIRING SCC41 WAS my Mt. Everest. It was the zenith of my career achievement, but my story didn't end there. There were many more mountains to climb.

What does digital TV, surveillance cameras, and cloud computing have in common? In my case, they marked the last chapter of my Motorola career.

Many of us remember the date of June 12, 2009 when the United States government mandated that all free over-the-air TV broadcasting had to go digital. The switchover from analog to digital broadcasting freed up valuable radio spectrum—the real estate in the air that television signals travel over. The U.S. government was considering making this spectrum available for use by cell phones and personal computers. As a result, industry consortium efforts sprang up to get ready to take advantage of this valuable resource.

One such alliance was called the *TV White Space Coalition*. I was assigned to work with the coalition as one of two Motorola representatives. The coalition was an industry partnership aimed at taking advantage of the newly available spectrum. The highlight of the assignment was that I got to work with industry powerhouses Google and Microsoft who were the chief movers behind the coalition. Unfortunately, the discussions dragged on for almost two years. Progress was frustrated by corporate egos and conflicting agendas. It was a case study in the entanglement of modern-day corporate relationships, where your partner could also be your customer, your supplier, and your competitor.

As the talks stalled, my job assignment changed once again. This time I landed in the Applied Research department focused on the development of video.

My new job was focused on video surveillance standards. Video was becoming an important tool to fight crime and terrorism and to aid in rescue efforts. Video surveillance was becoming the third eye that was watching everyone everywhere. A new technology called video analytics was emerging. Imagine being able to track the faces of suspects as they move through airports and public places, to instantaneously turn the camera to where a gunshot has been heard, or to be able to detect an illegal facility entry because the system detected that the camera's preset intrusion parameters were violated. Imagine doing all this without any human intervention. This was state-of-the-art research work.

I was enamored with the idea of using video technology to fight crime even though my job had more to do with directing the related standards strategy. At last, I was working on something remotely human! Then a wonderful opportunity came along.

The local police department (PD) had a trailer that had been used for demonstrating child-seat safety some years ago. After the program ended, the trailer was mainly used for storage. One of the police lieutenants came up with the idea to convert it into a mobile command center, complete with video and surveillance capabilities, to be used for such events as the annual summer festivals and occasional dignitary visits. The PD approached Motorola for assistance. It was to be a *pro bono* project, but it would give Motorola the opportunity to showcase its wireless and video technology and to be seen as a good corporate citizen in the community where we were headquartered. I was thrilled to be assigned to lead the project.

The PD wanted this to be a community project, so the local high school got involved. For one semester, we worked with students in an industrial design class to come up with a design for the interior space of the mobile unit. We had to deal with safety codes, heating and ventilation needs, power supply and lighting, and come up with a floor plan and furnishings that would be conducive to how the police do their surveillance and command-and-control work. The PD took me to see other crime scene investigation command vehicles. We also worked with the trucking contractor to remodel the trailer so that the video equipment could be transported securely. A renowned video company served as our consultants. In the end, I learned a great deal about state-of-the-art cameras, video surveillance, and how law enforcement personnel use both to fight crime.

My last hurrah was with a new business unit called Advanced Services that Motorola launched in 2010 to go beyond selling hardware to creating value-added services and solutions for our customers. I was responsible for figuring out how to create a hosted service for Computer Aided Dispatch (CAD) for police and emergency response personnel.

The buzzword in the late 2000s was cloud computing. Public Safety agencies were under tremendous cost-cutting pressure to do more with less. They were scrambling to find alternative solutions for their increasingly demanding computing needs. Cloud computing, where the computing equipment is purchased and maintained by a third party and stored elsewhere (in the cloud), sounded like the panacea to their problems. It would save them upfront capital money and ongoing expenses for staff and facilities. In return, the agencies would pay a monthly fee to the hosting company.

I was excited by my new assignment but making the business case work proved to be a lot harder than we thought. It would require huge capital investments on Motorola's part to go into the computer and applications hosting business. There were also colossal technical challenges to ensure sub-second response time required by these life-saving services. A 911 call couldn't tolerate any delays or failure-to-connect issues. The biggest hurdles, however, were the regulatory and security issues, as no precedent had been set for such an operational model—that of a private sector company hosting services for public safety agencies. I didn't get to see the launch of the public safety hosting business before I left Motorola.

During the four decades of my professional life, my career ran the gamut of technology development, people management, and business management. When people find out about my background, they are amazed at how I could perform and excel, not just once or twice, but over and over again, at highly technical jobs without any formal training. I look back at the surprising twists and turns in my career and the hurdles I had overcome and realize how far I had come. I think I can chalk it up to my determination to succeed, my openness to embrace change, my willingness to take risks, my ability to persevere, and my tough-as-nails work ethic. In everything I have done in my life, I've given it my all. I've done it through determination, sweat, and tears. I can truly say that in my career, every promotion, every award, and every accolade was hard earned.

30

The Bonus

BEFORE I WRAP up the roller-coaster tale of my Motorola journey, I would be remiss if I didn't mention one great benefit that I got out of my job, and that was the opportunity to travel and see the world.

During the twenty-plus years of my international assignments, I traveled to every corner of the world. My Joint Venture business development work and my Standards work took me to more countries than I can recall. During my expansive global travels, I visited most of the major cities in the United States and in Europe, parts of Latin America, and many cities in Asia.

By far, the most memorable trip I made was to the city of Luleå, in Sweden.

It was early in my standards job and I was attending a 3GPP (3G Partnership Program) meeting. The meeting was hosted by Ericsson, a Swedish company that provided telecommunications equipment. At every standards meeting, there was always a social function. The event served as an icebreaker and an opportunity for the meeting participants to mingle and network. Ericsson wanted to give their guests an unforgettable arctic experience.

The Swedish port of Luleå, at the northern end of the Gulf of Bothnia, is the largest town in Norrbotten County, the northernmost county of Sweden. It is the gateway to the mountain world of Lapland and the northern tundras. Luleå is only seventy miles from the Arctic Circle. It was my first trip to the top of the world.

On the day of the outing, we were suited up in winter gear supplied by our host. The garments were designed to protect us against the dangerously low Arctic temperatures. They looked like army fatigues that covered us from head to toe. After we were inspected to make sure that we were properly suited up, we climbed onto husky-pulled sleds, four to a sled. Determined not to miss anything, I took the front seat. Not smart. As we plowed through the wintry terrain, my face was pelted by prickly, icy snow driven by the onslaught of the wind.

But the view was breathtaking. Miles of virgin snow-decorated pine forests greeted us along the path. All was quiet except for the whistling of the wind and the barking of the dogs. I was transported to a different world, the world of pristine arctic wilderness. An hour into the ride, we stopped and made coffee in a roadside pit. Then we went inside a tepee to warm up. The coffee was watery and the tepee was smoke-filled, but we had warm conversations and hearty laughs.

The travel options for returning to the hotel were either by snowmobile or reindeer-pulled sleigh. I chose the snowmobile. I had never ridden on a snowmobile, but I decided there was no time like the present to try. Again, I opted to be in the front and I chose to ride by myself. The experience was magical. The snowmobile was surprisingly easy to control and the ride was exhilarating. We saw endless forest vistas, drove through open powder meadows, and experienced the famous "snow ghosts" that are formed when the wind blows the snow onto the trees. I was enchanted.

For the meeting banquet, we ate stir-fried reindeer meat and cloudberries while sitting on tree stumps inside a huge tepee. Yes, Luleå was one of my most unforgettable travel experiences.

Mark Twain once wrote, "Travel is fatal to prejudice, bigotry, and narrow-mindedness, and many of our people need it sorely on these accounts. Broad, wholesome, charitable views of men and things cannot be acquired by vegetating in one little corner of the earth all one's lifetime."

I look back at where I have been and I know Mark Twain is absolutely correct. Through my travels, I learned so much about the places and people that existed beyond my small world. Visiting places I had never been and learning about the history and culture of people I otherwise would never have had the chance to meet gave me fresh perspectives and new appreciation. Some enlightened me. Others stirred my soul. Many left lasting impressions.

I rode taxicabs in India that stopped at intersections where BMWs, scooters, cycle rickshaws, and rundown trucks competed for right of way with cows!

In Moscow while waiting in a long line to purchase our Big Macs at McDonald's, the police came over and asked if they could help us get to the front of the line for a fee!

In Mexico City I was fascinated by the different colors of the license plates and learned all about "day without a car," or "Hoy no Circula," where every car had to stay off the road one day a week to minimize the catastrophic level of air pollution.

I was sitting at an outdoor café in Bangalore at dusk, and watched in horror as the hotel staff sprayed the grounds with what I believed to be DDT, and a carpet of mosquitoes fell from the air onto my coffee.

In Tokyo, I was in awe of a nation so respectful of public cleanliness that an entire beachfront emptied out after a festival, without one hint of litter left behind because everyone took their trash home with them.

In Beijing, I entered the halls of the Forbidden City thinking of how the Empress Dowager spent her stormy days running China from behind the puppet Emperor Pu Yi.

While marveling at the Great Wall, I felt a deep sadness for the sacrifices of the laborers who constructed this amazing structure that can be seen from outer space.

In Bangalore, I was struck by the sight of a mother kneeling by the roadside begging, with her small baby laying on the dirt beside her, while the massive billboards of IBM and Oracle advertising the prosperity of technology flashed over her head.

I stood in the middle of red square in Moscow, and was moved to tears by its magnificence and the memory of the brutal and bloody events that took place there.

In Istanbul, I peeked into a shrouded prayer room hidden in the back, and was indignant to find out that it was reserved for women who were not allowed to pray openly in the mosque.

In Argentina, on a beautiful island called Borges Lagoa, I was amazed to find that the bottom of the world looked just like the top of the world, when I opened my hotel room window to a storybook-like alpine landscape that reminded me of Switzerland.

I watched Kabuki theatre in Japan, flamenco dancers in Argentina, and a bullfight in Spain. I saw many castles and cathedrals in Europe, and just as many shrines and temples in Asia. I took more river and canal cruises than I could count with my two hands.

The world is small, and people are alike no matter where you go. Traffic problems are the same in London, Mexico City, and Beijing. Parents in India, Brazil, and Sweden all want the same things for their children—a good education and a better life. We may have differences in religion, language, and skin color, but those only betray how similar we are beneath the surface. There is a certain human homogeneity in community, school, food, music, the arts, sports, and games that binds us together. The quest for love and happiness is the common denominator.

I am convinced that travel changes people. I feel so fortunate to have seen spectacular sights, walked on the streets of history, met remarkable people, tasted amazing local cuisine, and sampled local arts and festivities. I am certain they served to shape the person I am today, and I hope that means I am a bit wiser, humbler, and maybe more open-minded because I have seen more than my small part of the world.

Things become so much clearer when you put them down in writing. I used to begrudge the fact that I never had the luxury of pursuing the career of my dreams, but now I see that through my working journey, I was given opportunities beyond my wildest dreams.

Part Four

Finding my other Horse:
Lessons of the Heart

31

The Courage to Walk Away

FOR A LONG, long time, I consoled myself by saying of my accomplishments, "Two out of three isn't bad!" What I meant was, between motherhood, marriage and career, I was two for three. My job was great, my children were wonderful, but my marriage was in shambles.

I wrote in a wedding book once, "A good marriage can add so much to one's life. Everything is so much better when you have someone to share it with." But I knew that the converse was also true. A bad marriage can cause so much pain and so much harm.

I lived a life of secrecy for years, hiding from the world. I was ashamed of the choice I had made in my marriage. Andy and I couldn't have been more different in our upbringing, our personalities, our values, and what we wanted out of life. Our differences were staggering. We were continents apart in every aspect of our emotional and material wants and needs. If we had not been married, we wouldn't even have been casual friends. Our marriage was a mistake that I had made and allowed to continue for twenty-plus years because I lacked the courage to make the change we both needed.

History had repeated itself. I was living my mother's life. I could almost hear her saying, "You made your bed so you must lie in it."

My marriage became my bitter prison. I was angry all the time. I felt trapped. I was often despondent. Even the happiness I got from my children and the pride I got from my job couldn't pull me out of the despair that consumed me. Corrosive resentment filled my being. I saw no way out of my unhappy life.

So I hid from the world. I avoided making friends. I never joined any groups or participated in any activities. I didn't reach out to my parents or my siblings. I lived in the fake reality of a content if not happy marriage. The only person that knew about my situation was my friend Joanne.

Joanne was the wife of Sid, my colleague at REA. For whatever reason, Joanne took a liking to me the moment we met. She became my best friend and substitute family in America. She was the one who came to help me when Ryan was born. She was the "aunt" who brought gifts and birthday cakes to my children on holidays and birthdays. She was my shoulder to cry on during the dark days of my unhappy marriage and my painful divorce. Joanne told me that she saw the trouble in my marriage the moment she met me.

I think Andy also knew. He once told me, "I love you enough for the both of us." That simply doesn't work. Love has to be mutual. The basic elements of trust, respect, acceptance, and caring must exist for a marriage to prevail. A one-sided relationship never works.

In hindsight, I made so many mistakes:

I fell in love with the idea of getting married, not the person I was marrying.

I married Andy in the hope that I could "fix" him.

I looked to marriage to fill my own emptiness.

I thought that having children would keep us together.

I stayed in the marriage for the sake of the children.

I put the blame (and the responsibility) on myself to keep the marriage intact.

I was wrong on all counts. A bad marriage is as insidious as a slow brewing poison; indifference, bickering, and eventually disdain and hostility gradually eat away at any hope of happily-ever-after.

All my life I trusted in the Chinese values of loyalty and commitment. I knew that love and relationships require work. But if your relationship is unbalanced and one person is constantly hurting, how much is enough? How shattered would I allow myself to get before I accept that my marriage is leaving me damaged and broken?

I came to realize that my unhappy marriage was causing my children much pain. I wrestled with so many questions: Can I teach them how to have successful relationships if I am in a miserable one myself? How will my failure affect their own confidence in finding love and happiness? How will it affect their expectations about marriage and relationships?

So when did I know that breaking up was the right thing to do? It was a heart-wrenching decision to make. I went back and forth over it for years. But it was not until one day, as I sat inside my car in the garage with the engine running, that I came face to face with the fact that life was no longer worth living. My body ached with grief. Tears ran uncontrollably down my face. The pain was so intense, the unhappiness so unrelenting, and life seemed so utterly unbearable. As I contemplated suicide, I thought about what would be better for my children. I knew I had reached the utmost threshold of pain that I could endure. I knew that I must leave the marriage for my sake and the children's.

I filed for divorce. After a two-year bitter fight that involved money and custody (my daughter Megan was a minor at the time), at age forty-five I was once again on my own.

It was a painful watershed in my life. It was as if I had taken a pair of scissors and cut my family's history into pieces. I cried for months as I mourned the demise of our family unit. I wept for the death of my vows. I cried for my children that they would now become a statistic of a broken home. Most of all, I felt the weight of my failure. In what I regarded to be the single most important achievement in one's life, a happy and enduring marriage, I had failed.

The break-up of my marriage was very hard on my children. Overnight everything changed. It was as if their world had been torn apart. The crying and depression went on for a long time, more visibly for Megan, less so for Ryan, although I probably underestimated what my son went through.

Soon after the divorce, Ryan went off to college, and Megan and I were left to face the aftermath of the divorce with each other.

For years after the divorce, Megan was very angry with me. She was "Daddy's Girl", so she took it very hard. She blamed me for breaking up the family. She resented me for throwing her dad out of the house.

She was openly mean and sarcastic to me. She challenged everything I said. She criticized everything I stood for. She rebelled against decisions I made. She was convinced that money and success were disdainful goals because she believed that they were the cause of our break-up. She vowed never to be a corporate ladder climber like me.

This continued for over three years, until one day I decided that enough was enough. I sat her down and demanded answers.

"Why are you so angry with me? I know you hurt. I have been trying so hard to reach out to you, but you won't let me in. You have been so mean to me. I don't deserve it. I need you to tell me what you want me to do. Do you hate me so much that you don't want me in your life?"

Megan was in denial at first. Then she broke down. Yes, she was mad at me over the divorce. No, she didn't realize what she had been doing to me. Yes, she loved me and wanted me in her life.

We cried and hugged and cried some more. We agreed that going forward we needed to talk things over and be honest with our feelings. As Megan entered adulthood, she began to see things in a different light. She no longer held it against me for making the decision to walk away from an unhappy marriage. She even admired me for my courage and strength to make that tough decision so that I could have a chance to be happy again.

Years later I heard Megan make this remark: "I don't understand why people use things that happened to them as a child as a crutch for the rest of their lives. I am a child of divorce, and I don't feel that I got such a raw deal. That is just part of your past, so get over it." When I heard that, I knew she had healed.

The life of a single woman is hard. The life of a single mother is even harder. The day I got my divorce, I went to the hardware store and bought my first set of tools—a screwdriver, a portable drill, and a small hammer. That was my declaration of independence. I needed to reassure myself that I would be all right.

What was I afraid of? Strange as it sounds, I was terrified by the mundane and practical demands of running the household by myself. I had never used a tool, mowed the lawn, shoveled the snow, changed the filter, or lit the furnace. I had to learn to do a lot of things that my husband had done for me. I couldn't hire out every chore because money was also short.

I was paying off a second mortgage I had taken to purchase a townhouse for Andy. I was also paying two years of alimony. The children's college expense was coming up quickly. I had no family around to give me any help. The only person I could count on was me.

A great decision that I made around this time was to move my children back to a middle-class neighborhood close to where I worked. Part of the motivation was to return to a community with middle-class values. Our house in Hawthorn Woods was a big house but an unhappy home. It had more space than we needed, more yard than I cared to maintain, and it was deplete of the neighborly community that I craved. I wanted to get back to basics and downsize to a house that I could manage. I wanted my children to be able to walk to their friends' houses. I wanted to once again live in a neighborhood with block parties, 4th of July parades and park district activities.

To make a clean break, I decided to build a new house to mark my new beginning. It was one of the best decisions I ever made.

Driving to work one day I saw construction activities around a small patch of land about one mile from my office. The location was perfect. Both the high school and grade school was half a mile away. I stopped by to make inquiries and found that there were still lots available. It was going to be a very small subdivision of twenty-two homes. The builder was a custom builder who had built two other subdivisions in Rolling Meadows. I liked what I saw so I quickly signed on.

I had managed multi-million dollar projects at work, but a personal project like building my own house was much more overwhelming. Since I had no idea what kind of house I wanted to build, I studied a plan my builder provided so that I could have some idea of cost. For months, I pored over the blueprint. There were so many decisions to be made. From the layout of the floor plan to the materials, the choices were endless. I went to the brickyard to pick out the bricks I wanted for the facade of my house. I drove around many neighborhoods to get an idea of how the color of the bricks would work with the color of the roof that I had selected. I laid out hundreds of tiles on the showroom floor to decide what patterns and colors of tiles to use for my kitchen and baths. I drove my builder crazy by changing the layout of the kitchen at least nine times. Of all things, the most important to me was to have a large inviting kitchen where family and friends could gather. I love the kitchen I designed. It became the heart of our home.

My house had one idiosyncrasy. There were closets everywhere. A fanatic about storage, I pored over the blueprint for every unused nook and cranny and inserted storage closets wherever I found room. No, I wasn't a hoarder, but it was difficult for me to throw anything away!

I was hands-on with every decision, from the elevation of the roof down to the placement of the wall switches and the style of the doorknobs, the house was every inch mine.

Every lunch hour I could spare I drove to the construction site to watch the progress of my new home. It was exciting and fun and it distracted me from the pain of my divorce. I was so proud when we finally moved into our new house. It was a beautiful home. It became the symbol of a new beginning for me and for my kids.

Ryan and Megan entered new schools as a high school sophomore and a fourth grader respectively. We settled into a new kind of normalcy. I juggled the chauffeuring, cooking, cleaning, and yard maintenance while putting in long hours at work. I found doctors and dentists close by. The one-mile distance in my triangle of home, school, and work was the saving grace in my new role as a single parent. It allowed me to make quick runs to attend an activity in my children's school, take them to a dentist appointment, stop at the grocery store, and still be able to return to my office to put in significant time for my job.

My children and I had survived my divorce. I began to regain control of my life. Life was not perfect, but now we could go forward.

32

On My Own Again

CHILDREN ARE RESILIENT. Changing houses, starting new schools, and finding new friends didn't seem to faze them. Ryan and Megan thrived after we moved to our new house in Rolling Meadows. They loved their new schools and quickly made new friends. Our middle-class neighborhood had a large Asian population because of the good schools. Many of Ryan and Megan's friends were children of immigrants and shared the same strong old-world values. All of them were from hard-working middle-class families who believe in education and personal achievements. We felt like we belonged.

Ryan took up tennis. Having a working mom meant that my children had to figure out a lot of things themselves, as I wasn't always available to take them where they wanted to go. Ryan enjoyed tennis so much that every afternoon after school, he walked to the local bus-stop with a portable stool. There he sat and waited for the bus that only stopped every hour on the hour to take him to the Tennis Club. Such sacrifices taught him the value of "if you want something, you will find a way to get it."

Ryan made friends easily. He joined a wide variety of extracurricular activities, including the Thespians and the Debate Team. He even became the vice-president of the Chess Club. Ryan blossomed into a fun-loving teenager with a great sense of humor. One of the favorite things that he liked to do with his friends was movie making at home. These were home movies with an attempt at script writing and directing. Ryan's friend Tim, who was a talented writer, would create scripts of hilarious short features where Ryan would play the leading role. I recall one such movie where Ryan was going around the house with a cane pretending to be a blind man and knocking down everything that stood in his way. Real funny!

Megan developed a passion for dancing. When she was little, I put her in ballet lessons at age three because I had a feeling it would help her overcome her shyness. I would dress her in full dance gear complete with bandanas and leg warmers. She looked like a mini Jane Fonda. Unfortunately, she was a reluctant participant. She would stand frozen in the middle of the dance floor while the whole class danced around her. It took six months, but eventually she came around. Before the first year was up, she was eagerly looking forward to her dance lessons every Saturday morning. Through the years, we enjoyed watching Megan perform in many dance recitals and competitions. I even signed her up as a Junior Lovable to perform at the Bulls basketball games.

Even though my children were thriving, being a single parent was exhausting and lonely. In spite of how busy I was, I found the loneliness unbearable. Many evenings after the children had gone to sleep, I sat in my room and disintegrated into a tearful mess. On the outside, I put up an appearance of having the strength of steel. On the inside, the gaping hole in my heart left me drained and empty. I was hanging on just enough to make it through another day.

During one of my many business trips, while I was on a plane to somewhere, I felt an aching so strong that I broke down and wept. At 33,000 feet in the air, I held out my hand to God and asked for his help. It was a daring thing to do. I hadn't gone to church in years. I wasn't sure that God would listen to someone like me who had abandoned her Christian beliefs since her youth. I wasn't even sure which God I was praying to. But there sitting with my Sony ear-buds on to hide my somewhat bizarre behavior, I felt a divine presence comforting me. In the quiet of my head, I heard an inner voice speak to me. I knew what I needed to do.

In my life, I have learned well that God only helps those who help themselves. I knew that I needed to take the initiative. In business, we create long-term business plans. Why not do it for my personal life? On a cocktail napkin, I began to write out my personal five-year plan.

I scribbled down everything I wanted to accomplish in the next five years to bring fun and purpose into my life. I wrote down everything I had always wanted to do but never got around to. The list included learning to ride a bike, swim, play golf, play bridge, and social dancing. It was an ambitious list. I made conservative goals by scheduling them over a five-year period.

In my quest for friendship and community, I started to go to church and made a conscious effort to find new friends and reconnect with old ones. I bought a bike and got up enough courage to teach myself to ride around the block. I even tried to rollerblade with Ryan and Megan holding me up on each side. I met up with some friends from work and learned to play bridge. I even tried my hand at playing golf, in spite of the fact that I didn't like spending hours in the sun.

To my dismay, I discovered that the social world was made for couples; a single woman inevitably posed a threat. When I tried to make friends with other singles from work, I was disappointed to find that they were more interested in looking for a man than developing meaningful friendships with me. I tried the bar scene, but after just one trip to a nearby tavern with a co-worker, I found the experience degrading and a complete waste of my time. I hated the undignified flirting and the superficial conversations. I was not interested in putting myself into a line-up of desperate single women waiting to be picked up by some random guy looking for his next hook-up. In my fantasy, there would be a Harrison Ford or a Richard Gere searching for me across a crowded room. But all I saw were pudgy middle-aged men wearing gold chains over white turtlenecks whose goal was to hunt for their next one-night-stand. I tried a couple of blind dates arranged by friends and acquaintances. I even joined a dating service called *It's Just Lunch*. I met many frogs and a handful of potential princes, but finding "the one" was as elusive as finding the proverbial needle in the haystack.

I began to lose hope. Maybe "the one" doesn't really exist. Maybe true love doesn't happen to everyone. Maybe everyone settles. Maybe I am trying too hard. They say you have to learn to love yourself first. Have I done that? Should I stop waiting for someone to make me happy and try to make myself happy? Do I know what makes me happy?

33

The Dance

THEY SAY THAT you'll find what you're looking for when you're not looking. Five years after my divorce, when I was least expecting it, I met the love of my life.

The year 1999 was a very significant year. Macau, my birthplace, reverted to China after 329 years of Portuguese rule. The Portuguese occupation of Macau had been the longest European settlement in Asia. I turned fifty that year.

On a chilly Sunday afternoon in late February, I walked into a Filipino Dance Studio and into my destiny. A month ago, I had run into a friend at work by the name of Tricia. Tricia and I worked together when I first joined Motorola, but after several job changes, we had lost track of each other. I had not seen Tricia for a decade, and we were eager to play catch-up. When she told me that she had taken up ballroom dancing, I wanted to know more. Learning to dance was one of the to-dos on my five-year plan, but I didn't know how to get started. I asked Tricia for pointers on where to go. She invited me to join her at a local dance studio that Sunday.

The studio was located on the second floor of a two-story commercial building in a western suburb. The dance practice took place in a large sun-lit room with hardwood floors and mirror-lined walls. Music was playing out of a boom box. There were about forty people on the dance floor dancing to the beat of some Latin music. I soon learned that this music went by the names of Cha-cha, Rumba, Waltz, Tango, and Merengue. It was an open-dance format. Everyone just danced to their skill level and when needed, asked for help from others who had more experience. It was all about just jumping in and doing it without formal instructions. I quickly warmed up to the idea. Everyone appeared to be having a lot of fun.

Since this was my first time at the studio, the instructor came over to help me with some beginner's steps. The first dance I learned was the Cha-Cha: Back step, cha cha cha; forward step, cha cha cha. The music was wonderful. The environment was unintimidating. I thought to myself, *I could do this!*

The dance started at around noon and went to five in the afternoon. I was first introduced to a friendly guy named Eli. Eli danced with me for about fifteen minutes and we went for a soda break. As we were standing around the refreshment table, Eli asked me what I did for a living. I told him I was in Engineering Standards. Eli turned to a guy standing behind us and declared, "Clark is an engineer too!" I glanced over and saw a tall, medium-built Filipino man with a strong jaw and thick dark hair. He had deep-set brown eyes and a full mouth. He smiled at me and asked me if I would like to dance.

Clark was gentle and patient and made me feel completely at ease despite my lack of natural ability to learn the dance moves. About an hour into the dance practice, we stopped for lunch. Everyone had brought food for a potluck lunch. Clark was a real gentleman and brought me my food. We sat down for lunch together and began to talk. The conversation flowed effortlessly. We exchanged business cards. After lunch, we resumed our dance practice.

In the studio, it was customary to change partners so that everyone could take turns learning from different people with different skill levels and styles. But Clark and I never did. For the next four hours, we danced like there was nobody else in the room. A friend of Clark's remarked to us, "You guys looked like you were in a trance." No doubt, she saw that something had happened between the two of us on that dance floor.

In the middle of a dance, the Tango, Clark said to me, "Look at me." It was meant to be an instructional remark. To properly dance the Tango, you must establish a connection with your partner; you need to look at your partner. I looked into Clark's eyes and something magical happened. The look went straight from his eyes into my heart. I shuddered with a strange intoxicating sensation. My head was spinning. Was it the music or the rhythm of the dance that made me feel lightheaded? Was it the way he held me that sent my heart pounding? Was it something else that I couldn't explain? I was lost in the dance.

The next day Clark sent me an email. It was a playful message about how my contact information had become "a standard" in his address book. I would soon learn about Clark's sense of humor. It's a little corny but very endearing. It was obvious that he was attempting a play on words with my job title. I was surprised that he would contact me so quickly. He invited me to a dance practice that following Friday. And by the way, he added, why don't we have dinner before that?

I called my friend Tricia and pelted her with questions. "Do you know anything about this guy? Do you know if he is married?"

"No, but I didn't see a ring on his finger, and he has never come to practice with anybody," Tricia told me.

That was all I needed to hear. I accepted his invitation.

We met in a restaurant by the studio called the Terrace. I found out more about Clark, a lot more. He dropped the bombshell that he was married, but the marriage was the verge of dissolution. He had been planning for a divorce. I didn't know how to react. I had just met this man. We hardly knew each other. It was not proper for me to push for more answers. Yet through the dinner that night, it was obvious that we both felt a strong connection.

On the way back to the car, we saw a sign that said *30 acres for sale*. "Where are the thirty acres?" Clark asked, as he grabbed my hand and pulled me closer to look at the property. It was a feigned excuse to get me close to him. And then he kissed me. I felt a tingling sensation going through my veins, traveling all the way from my head to my toes. I shuddered uncontrollably. I knew then that I had fallen in love with this man I hardly knew.

I was falling hard for Clark. We talked almost every day on the phone. We met the next Sunday morning and had breakfast at McDonalds. Three weeks later as we were hanging up on the phone, he whispered the words "I love you."

"It's too soon," I told him. "You can't mean it. You hardly know me."

My heart soared at his declaration of love, but my head told me that I needed to be cautious. We had only seen each other three times. Was he a playboy? Did he say this to every woman he met? And yet there was something very sincere and vulnerable about this man. I felt I could really believe him.

As things turned out, he really meant it. It was love at first sight. We did fall in love the day we met. Our love was not only real; it was intense and consuming. We not only became lovers; we became best friends. If there is such a thing as soul mates, Clark is mine.

Handsome, confident, generous, opinionated, loyal, stubborn and proud—Clark was exactly what the doctor ordered.

If I could bottle the first six months of our romance, it would be an intoxicating brew. Anyone who has ever experienced an intense relationship knows what I am talking about. I woke up in the morning thinking about him. I went to bed at night dreaming about him. At work, I found it difficult to concentrate. I walked around with a silly grin on my face. We talked at least three, four times on the phone regardless of how busy our workday was. We couldn't wait to see each other at the end of each day. We met up for lunch breaks in the park. We held hands while taking long walks. We stole kisses in movie theaters. I wrote intimate letters to Clark. He bought Hallmark cards of romantic poetry for me. There was a huge aching hole in my heart before Clark came along. A divine hand had reached down and closed up the hole, and filled its space with sweet joy and contentment.

In the months to come, I learned a lot more about this man who came from nowhere and turned my world upside down. Clark was born and raised in Manila, the capital city of the Philippines. The second of five children, he was the oldest male and became the patriarch of the family after his father died. Clark was well loved and respected by everyone around him. His family and friends held him in the highest esteem. From financial matters to home improvement, they looked up to him for advice, help, and support, as he was always ready to lend a hand. Academically, Clark was a gifted student who moved quickly through the school system. At age twenty, he graduated with honors with a degree in Mechanical Engineering from the Mapúa Institute of Technology, the top engineering university in the Philippines. He immigrated to the United States in 1972, the same year that I graduated from college.

Up until the time we met, Clark's social circle had been almost 100 percent Filipino. He was civic-minded and held leadership positions in a number of Filipino organizations. His social life revolved around his family, his community, and a close-knit group of friends who were exclusively Filipino. Ironically, Clark was the first Filipino I had ever met. So fate had something to do with the two of us being in the same place at the same time that February afternoon in 1999.

Because we are both immigrants, we share the same old world values, such as the importance of family, loyalty, respect, and work ethics, to name a few. Our personalities are similar in many ways. We are perfectionists in almost everything we do. We are both stubbornly proud and self-reliant. The flip side is that we are also extremely pig-headed. What saves us is the deep love and respect we have for each other, so much so that it always trumps our pride. We are two people who learned from our failed marriages and resolved never to make the same mistakes again.

Clark and I shared many passions, including home improvement, photography, travel, and food, but by far the greatest love we shared was dancing. Dancing was how we began. I believe that dancing is one of the best activities a couple can do together. I am thrilled that American TV shows like "Dancing with the Stars" have ignited new interest in ballroom dancing in America. When two people dance, the hold, the grace, the unison transports you to a different place. The tempo and the beat of the music heighten all of your senses and make you feel alive. Partner dancing requires a physical and emotional connection. It is not surprising that people fall in love while dancing.

We love every kind of dance: the sultry Salsa, the edgy Tango, the romantic Rhumba, the elegant Waltz, and the fun Cha-cha are all our favorites. One dance we are fascinated with is the Argentine Tango. It is a dance that embodies beauty, passion, and drama. The music is mournful and stirring, and the movement is at once elegant and electrifying. Couples who dance the Argentine Tango cling to each other and become fused together like the braided trunks of a money tree. You must be one with your partner to feel where his body goes so that yours can follow. It's the ultimate couple's dance. One of our dreams is to one day go to Buenos Aires and spend a whole month watching and learning the Argentine Tango.

People tell us that we are beautiful dancers; that they love to watch us dance. I don't think we have the best techniques. We don't get in the practice time we need to become excellent technical dancers. However, I do think that we have great chemistry when we dance. I believe that chemistry is what makes the dance beautiful.

I am so grateful to have found "true love" at a late stage in my life. It shows that this wonderful blessing can happen to anyone. I think it all starts with being open and ready for love to come.

34

For Better or Worse

A YEAR AFTER we met, Clark lost his job.

He had just purchased a townhouse and was settling down to having his own place after his divorce. At the company where he worked, he was Vice President of Engineering. He was doing well at the job, so the dismissal came as a complete shock. The company was a family-owned business where a power struggle took place between two siblings. There was a winner and a loser. Clark, who was part of the old regime, became a victim of the family feud.

It was at the time of another mild recession and jobs for senior level managers were scarce. Clark had never been in this position before. Being an extremely proud man, I could see the devastating effect this had on him. He became very sensitive to the most casual remarks. If I didn't ask about his job search, he felt that I didn't care. If I asked too often, he became irritated that I was putting too much pressure on him. I felt like I was walking on eggshells. But in spite of it all, I stood fast by him. I knew he needed me more than ever during this time, even though he tried to push me away. He told me that I probably wouldn't want to marry him now that he was unemployed. I told him that I would marry him tomorrow if he would ask me.

Clark was one of the most hard-working people I knew. He was not going to just sit around waiting for the next job to fall into his lap. Besides pumping out dozens of resumes and applications each week, he immediately looked for a stopgap job that would bring in some money and allow him to keep busy. A friend suggested becoming a mortgage loan processor. The job involves preparing the paperwork for applicants for a new or refinanced mortgage and getting a commission from the mortgage lender. Interest rates were going down; so many people were refinancing their houses.

Still, it was not easy to start over. To make money from mortgage loans you must bring in new clients. Clark was not used to making cold sales calls. I could see that he felt humiliated. I did my best to encourage him so I made it into something that we would do together. I would design and print the flyers advertising his service, and we would go around the neighborhood stuffing mailboxes. On one unforgettable afternoon, it was pouring rain and we were cold and drenched by the time we finished. As we drove home, Clark realized that he had lost his eyeglasses. They were expensive prescription trifocals and Clark had just purchased them a month ago. We retraced our path through the neighborhood, but the eyeglasses were nowhere to be found. He had not made a penny that day, but instead he had lost a pair of eyeglasses costing over $400.

It was a low point. We went home and curled up in each other's arms. I felt tears on our cheeks, his and mine. I wept because I knew how much he was hurting. This wonderful man whom I loved so much would never allow me to support him financially. He would make it on his own if it killed him.

Seven months after Clark lost his job, he found a job in St. Louis. He was so excited. There was really nothing to discuss because his mind was already made up. He would move any place if it meant that he would work again. He was hired as the Engineering Manager for a family-owned company that made food preparation equipment for large fast-food chains such as Taco Bell and Burger King. He would be getting back to his field of expertise. He would be an engineer again.

Thus began our lives as a commuting couple, and it would last for four and a half years. Every Friday Clark would drive the three hundred miles from St. Louis to Chicago to spend the weekend with me. Once or twice a month I would fly to St. Louis to spend the weekend at his apartment. A year later, we bought a house in a picturesque little town called Creve Coeur. I really wanted to make the whole commuting thing work. I wanted Clark to feel that he could put his heart and soul into his new job, and the house would allow him to have a sense of commitment.

Our house in St. Louis was a modest three-bedroom two-bath 1950s-era ranch style home on half an acre. It had beautiful hardwood floors, large bay windows, and great light. The previous owners were researchers from mainland China who had worked at Washington University nearby. They had not been very good with the upkeep of the property. The house was in need of both repairs and updating. The yard was overgrown.

We spent many weekends clearing the yard and turning it into a beautiful outdoor space. We cleared out all the overgrowth under the pine trees and Clark planted ground covers with little blue flowers. We both love day lilies, so we planted different varieties with vibrant colors everywhere in the yard. We hung wind chimes on the old tree that formed a canopy over the deck. We power-washed the deck, bought an outdoor grill, and created a seating area with a small glass table and two cast iron chairs. Many evenings we sat outside listening to the wind chimes and enjoying the tranquility of the quiet neighborhood.

Inside the house, we took on a titanic renovation project that involved opening the kitchen to the family room to create an inviting open floor-plan. The kitchen got a makeover with new cabinets, granite counter tops, stainless steel appliances, and ceramic tiles. We created an enormous island and a breakfast nook by reconfiguring the space and relocating doors and windows. It took five months during which we didn't have the use of a working kitchen, but when it was done, it was beautiful. We did it all by ourselves spending most of our weekends working on the house. All our sweat didn't return a great deal of equity, however. By the time we sold the house because of the downturn in the real estate market, we barely broke even. But the project brought us even closer together. It will always be a fond memory for us.

It was not all work all the time. We had a lot of fun going around the St. Louis area trying out the local restaurants, farmers markets, and even wine tasting in small vineyards we never imagined existed in Missouri. We found our favorite Sushi, Thai and Vietnamese restaurants. We went to the

Fox Theatre whenever a new show came to town. We even traveled to Branson and Lake of the Ozarks for small excursions. Every weekend was like a vacation. During the week, we talked everyday on the phone. Sometimes we would even watch a show together by tuning in to the same TV station and exchanging commentaries over the phone. In a word, we were shameless romantics. We made the relationship work in spite of the distance.

It was during the second year of Clark's stay in St. Louis that he proposed to me. Living apart didn't deter us from making a life together, but as a commuting couple, we avoided the subject of marriage. So the proposal took me by surprise. As of today, it was still the biggest surprise that Clark was able to pull off.

It was September 2002. Megan was entering her second year at Indiana University. I was in a funk because I really missed her. Ryan had already finished college, started his job with Motorola, and moved into his own condo. Megan was my baby, and I really felt a sense of loss when she left for school. Clark suggested that we take a mini vacation to chase away my blues. He booked a trip to Los Cabos, Mexico, a holiday town.

The Hilton Resort in Los Cabos had just opened. The property was breathtaking. We had a beautiful room with a gorgeous view. The first day we were there, we took it easy by spending most of our time at the infinity pool with a swim-up bar. We ordered nachos and Pina Coladas by the pool. It was heavenly.

By the time dinnertime came along, I was not in the least bit hungry. Clark insisted however, that we should dress up and go to dinner, as it was our first night there. I reluctantly agreed. As we walked into the Frontera dining room, I thought it was rather strange that there was nobody in the dining room. All of the guests were seated outside on the terrace. The captain led us to a table in the center of the room. I was still looking over the menu when he came back with an array of hors d'oeuvres. He told us they were compliments of the chef. *Very nice*, I thought. *What wonderful hospitality!*

Clark ordered two glasses of red wine. I protested a little because I don't drink wine, but I didn't want to spoil his fun. As I sipped my wine, I noticed that the bottom of the glass looked cloudy, but I thought I should keep it to myself. As I continued to sip my wine, something was obviously not right. There was definitely something in my glass. That something was more than a speck of dirt. It was an engagement ring!

As I let out a small cry, "There is a ring in my drink!" Clark fell on one knee. He fished out the ring and placed it on my finger. The captain came over to congratulate us. I was wiping tears of joy when he brought out a display of petite cakes and chocolates signed with a large raspberry sauce heart, "Compliments of the Chef." He beamed. Clark had arranged this whole thing with the captain and the kitchen. He had pulled off a huge surprise and an unforgettable proposal.

In the movie, "Shall we dance?" Richard Gere asks Susan Sarandon, who plays his wife in the movie, "Why do people get married?" Susan's answer goes something like this: People marry because we need a witness to our lives. There are so many people on this planet that one life is so insignificant. But when you get married, you are promising your partner that you will care about every little thing that happens to him. In other words, you will be there to bear witness to his life so that it will not go unnoticed.

Clark is the witness to my life. Through good times and bad, happiness and sadness, defeats and triumphs, he is there by my side. We learned to dance together, to taste new foods together, to travel the world together, and to dream big dreams together. The notion of time simply disappears when we talk for hours about nothing. Our hands automatically touch whenever we walk. We are each other's biggest fans. We make each other laugh.

In Clark, I see the man I have been waiting for all my life. I want to be forever young in his eyes. I want to grow old in his arms.

On June 8, 2003, four years after we met, in a small chapel in Naperville, Illinois, in the presence of a hundred friends and relatives, we exchanged our wedding vows.

Our wedding party consisted of our six children—three boys and three girls. My brother Jimmy walked me down the aisle. Jimmy's children, Victoria and Alex, acted as flower girl and ring bearer. Our wedding ceremony was filled with rituals and symbolism. To honor Clark's heritage, I incorporated Filipino traditions into our ceremony. I chose the *rope and veil* ceremony, as it symbolizes the joining and shielding of the couple and their relationship. I also designed a unity candle ceremony in which all of our children took part. One by one, they walked up to the altar and lit their candles. Then Clark and I lit our candles, and together, the eight of us joined in lighting the unity candle, symbolizing our commitment to unite as a new family. We then held hands and recited The Lord's Prayer. For the blessing, I chose a reading of the Apache blessing.

Now you will feel no storms,
For each of you is shelter for the other,
Now you will feel no cold,
For each of you is warmth to the other,
Now there's no loneliness,
For each of you is companion to the other,
You are still two persons,
And now there is only one life before you.
Go this day to your dwelling place
And enter into your days together.
May your days be good and long upon the earth.

It rained all day! Instead of outdoor pictures by the flowerbeds and along the river walk like we had planned, we had the most unique wedding pictures taken in the rain under a black-and-white golf umbrella. As a couple who had faced many challenges together, we had learned to embrace whatever came along. Certainly, we were not going to let the rain dampen our perfect day. As far as we were concerned, the heavens rained blessings on our union all day.

At our reception, the song we chose for our first dance was "Could I Have This Dance for the rest of my Life" by Anne Murray. We couldn't think of a better song to mark the beginning of our life together.

We officially became the Brady Bunch. We had no problem blending our family of eight—Clark's four children and my two children, who were supportive of us from the start. Over time, we grew to be a big, happy family. Over the past decade since we met, we celebrated many holidays and special occasions, and saw the weddings of our children and births of our grandchildren. I couldn't be happier with how things have turned out. I am grateful to our children for their love and support. I know that our closeness as a blended family is more the exception than the rule. I don't take our blessing for granted.

After the wedding, Clark went back to St. Louis while I continued to live in Chicago. We would live as a commuting couple for another three years. The separation was difficult. We did everything possible to be together. Sometimes we would meet each other half way around the world. When I went to Berlin for work, Clark joined me there. When Clark had to travel to China, I flew there to be with him.

As much as we tried hard to make the long-distance marriage work, Clark and I wanted so much to be together for good. Into the fifth year of his St. Louis commute, I decided that I needed to work on bringing him home. I started looking at jobs in the Chicago area for Clark. This was 2006 and the economy was once again slowing. Jobs were not plentiful and Clark's expertise in fast-food restaurant equipment was a niche. Not to be discouraged, I began forwarding Clark job postings that looked like a good fit for his skills. I knew my husband was a talented engineer with superb manufacturing expertise and unmatched work ethics. I knew that if he could only get the interview, he would have a good chance of getting the job.

One day on Monster.com, I found a job posting by Sears Holdings for an Engineering Manager for the Sears Kenmore line of small kitchen appliances. Sears Holdings is a retail conglomerate operating some 4,000 stores under different retail banners nationwide. The Kenmore brand of household appliances is one of Sears' strongest brands. The posting screamed perfect match for Clark's skills. What's the difference between a consumer kitchen appliance and a commercial restaurant appliance? I thought that it would be an ideal job for Clark.

After a bit of nudging, Clark agreed to apply. We couldn't believe it when he received a response from Sears a few days later asking him to fly to Chicago for an interview. The following Friday, Clark came home for the interview. A week later, they offered him the job.

Our world exploded. Bells rang. Angels sang. Everything had happened so fast. The dream that I had dreamt for four long years had finally come true. Best yet, I had the privilege of acting as Clark's "headhunter." I was bringing my husband home!

Two weeks later, Clark was driving home from St. Louis to take his new job with Sears Holdings. We made a trip back to St. Louis a month later to collect his clothing and a few important personal belongings. We gave away all the furniture and a great deal of the household items. We hired a realtor to have the house sold. Nothing mattered except to get Clark home as soon as possible. At long last, we would begin our lives as husband and wife living under one roof.

Clark loved his new job. A very gifted engineer with great sensibilities for style and design, his new job as Group Manager for the Kenmore line of microwave ovens, food processors, coffee makers … suited him perfectly. He was responsible for the new lineup of products that came out in the spring of every year. Besides overseeing the design and engineering of the appliances, he was also responsible for the quality of the products. For this reason, he traveled five times a year to China to inspect the factories and oversee the manufacturing process. His travels to China sparked his interest in learning Mandarin and Chinese customs. It brought us even closer together.

Bringing Clark home completed my happiness. Our love has endured the tests of time, fortunes, and distance, and has defied the odds of family ties. In the fourteen years we have been together, not much has changed from the rush of new love we felt right from the start. We still hold hands when we walk down the street. Clark still feeds me the first bite of my favorite food. We still kiss each other good morning and good night. I once heard Julia Roberts say on the Oprah show that her husband still takes her breath away. That is how I feel about Clark. Sometimes I catch a glimpse of Clark and say to myself, "What an elegant, beautiful man I married." His thoughtfulness, generosity, humor, and strength still blow me away.

35

My Father's Gift

IN THE WINTER of 2003, my father's illness brought me and Clark an unexpected gift.

I once read that prejudice is not born of evil, but of ignorance. We all have prejudices because we don't know any better. We are often taught prejudice by those whom we love and respect. We accept prejudice because our family and our peers tout it as the norm. We are conditioned to stereotyping because we have been desensitized to the evil of judging people by their skin color, ethnic origin, or whatever biases that have been passed down through generations and over time.

My father did not like Clark. He had never met Clark. He had no idea who Clark was and what he did for a living. It was simply blind prejudice. When I first told my father about Clark, I knew I had to mention his ethnicity. I wanted so much for my parents to be happy for us. But it was not to be. The minute I mentioned that Clark was Filipino, my parents wasted no time in letting me know how unhappy they were with my choice.

In Hong Kong and Macau, most of the maids, drivers, security guards and other domestic workers are Filipinos. Both my sister and my brother have employed Filipino maids for decades. Each weekend in Hong Kong, you will find hundreds of Filipino maids gathered at public places to exchange news from home. It is a sight that reinforces the stereotype that *all* Filipinos are servants. To be fair, most Hong Kong/Macau people have never met Filipinos who are successful doctors, lawyers, engineers, and businessmen—and there are plenty around the world—to help shatter the stereotype.

A week after I told my parents about Clark, my phone rang. It was my father, who had never called me on the phone since I had left home to come to America. He came straight to the point.

"Your mother couldn't sleep since your last call. Your news has caused her grave misery. She is so unhappy with your choice of a partner. We want you to know that we love you, and that you will always be welcome in our home, but don't bring Clark. If our friends find out that you are dating a Filipino, we will be so humiliated."

I didn't speak to my parents for a long time after my father's call. I was so angry that he didn't give Clark a chance or even attempt to get to know him. I just *knew* that if my father would only give him a chance, he would find out what a wonderful person Clark was. He would see that Clark was smart and accomplished, and that he was a man of strong character and family values. More importantly, Clark was the man I loved. If my father loved me, he should have looked past Clark's race and skin color. But instead, he wanted to have nothing to do with Clark. When Clark and I got married, I made sure that I send my parents an invitation. I wanted them to know that I chose my happiness over their prejudice.

Three months after Clark and I got married, I received news that my father was very ill. All my anger dissipated and I flew home to be by his side. As I opened the door to his hospital room, I saw a frail man lying in bed with tubes coming out of every part of his body. My father, who was once one of the most handsome men I had ever known, was skin and bones. When he saw me, he signaled me to come closer. He smiled at me and said, "Ah-Bing, my beautiful daughter!" At that moment, all was forgiven. The anger I had held in my heart for so long melted away. I fought back tears to put on a cheerful happy face. "It's good to see you, Ah-Ba."

He was suffering from blockages in the veins to his heart and complications in his kidneys. He had to undergo dialysis every three days, which I could see was extremely painful. He complained that his body hurt all over because he was all bones. Mealtime was a real challenge; he refused to eat because nothing tasted good to him anymore.

I visited him in the hospital every day with my sister Amy. There was not much I could do for my father except bring him food and encourage him to eat. Most days we just sat and made small talk. His skin was very dry, so I gently rubbed lotion over his arms and hands to soothe the dryness. He told me that it felt good.

I left after two weeks, as I needed to get back to work, and my father was neither improving nor deteriorating. Three weeks later, he passed away.

When I came home for my father's funeral, I brought Clark with me. This would be the first time my family met Clark. I decided that I would make the statement to introduce Clark as my husband and it would be up to them whether to accept him.

We got home on the day of the wake. Clark and I booked ourselves into a hotel instead of staying with my mother. I was expecting things to be chaotic and they were. My family had never been through a funeral before, and there were many details to attend to.

My sister Amy was fussing over the logistics of who, what, when, and where as if she was tackling the most serious assignment. Which suit should father be buried in? What are the seating arrangements at the visitation hall? How will all the flower arrangements fit into the room? How many tables should we reserve for dinner? I watched and understood. My sister was closest to my father. His death was most devastating to her. She was numbing her grief with busyness.

I introduced Clark to everyone, but their attention was focused on the funeral arrangements, which turned out to be the best thing. At the wake, my mother and we children sat on the front row to receive friends and relatives who came to pay their last respects. In accordance with Chinese customs, every time a new visitor came in, we had to stand up and return the bows. So the whole evening was spent in a ritual of standing up, bowing, and sitting down, only to stand up again when the next round of guests came along.

It is the Chinese custom for the children to sit next to the surviving parent according to their birth order. It is also the Chinese custom that the male children have higher status over the female children. As I was the second daughter in a family of three boys and two girls, I had the lowest rank in the seating arrangements. Clark sat next to me, and together we occupied the last two seats in the front row.

I was proud to be presenting Clark as my husband. He looked so Chinese as he sat next to me performing his duties as my father's son-in-law. Even our wreath bore his name. It said, "To my Father-in-Law. Respectfully, son-in-law Clark and daughter Yuen-Bing." It was ironic that because this was a male-dominated society, I had to be represented by my husband. Even the flower wreath that I dedicated to my father couldn't be in my name. It had to be from the son-in-law whom he never wanted to meet.

My father's burial place was in a well-known Chinese cemetery where my grandparents were also buried. It was a well-chosen lot on a hillside next to a Chinese pavilion. To get to the burial lot, we had to walk down some very steep stairs with no hand railings. The sand-covered steps were treacherous. My brother Jack led the way holding the picture of my father. Clark held my mother's hand as she walked down the stairs. I walked behind my mother and Clark. I was happy to see my mother accepting Clark's help. He was very gentle with her. She was leaning on him as they walked silently down the dusty stairs to the burial lot.

Weddings and funerals are the occasions that bring families together. Following the funeral there were a number of family dinners and gatherings. Everyone got to meet Clark. Again, the spotlight was not on my husband but rather the life and death of my father. It turned out to be the best circumstance to introduce Clark to my family. Because of that trip, the wall that had separated Clark from my family was torn down. No one ever mentioned Clark's ethnicity again. Clark became my mother's favorite son-in-law because he always visited her whenever he traveled to China for work. Because Clark spoke no Chinese, it forced my mother to recall the English she had learned as a child when she went to an English-speaking school. She was rather proud of herself.

So this was my father's gift to me—the gift of reconciliation. His death provided the opportunity for me to bring Clark into the family. I know my father loved me. I know that he would have loved Clark if he had known him. I am so glad that I had the chance to make up with him before he died. I am so grateful that it didn't become a source of regret that I would have had to endure for the rest of my life.

36

Sunrise, Sunset

WHEN RYAN GRADUATED from the University of Illinois in Champaign-Urbana at age twenty-one with an undergraduate degree in Electrical Engineering, he gave me a picture frame with this inscription.

"Through All The Hard Times You Believed In Me And Helped Me Believe In Myself. Today We Graduated Together."

The inscription moved me to tears. Ryan and I had been through a lot together. He gave me more love, pride, and joy than any mother could ever ask for. We have a special bond. He is my first-born, and in many ways, he taught me how to be a mother. We have similar personality traits: sense of duty, empathy for others, and loyalty to family and friends. True to the Chinese name I gave him, he is thoughtful, loving, and generous. I have never met another person who tries harder to always do the right thing.

After the divorce, Ryan became the man around the house. I came to rely on him for chores and mechanical things that my female brain couldn't comprehend. Without his father around, he figured things out on his own and he never complained about the extra responsibilities. The divorce hastened his growing up and bolstered his already mature nature.

For college Ryan chose to attend the Engineering School at the University of Illinois in Champaign (U of I or UIUC) majoring in Electrical Engineering. Ryan knew very early that he wanted to be an engineer. The influence could have come from my brother Jimmy who was an electrical engineer, or it could have been his love for technology and electronic gadgets. UIUC was a top engineering school with a reputation that rivaled MIT. For budgetary reasons I had asked Ryan to limit his choice of college to Illinois schools. He decided on the U of I because of its excellent reputation, even though he knew that the curriculum would be tough. The pressure didn't come from me. My mantra had always been "give it your best and live up to your potential." I was really proud of Ryan when he decided that he wouldn't take the easy way out. I was even more proud when he was accepted into UIUC.

Like most top engineering schools, U of I was very demanding. On the first week of college, the professor told the incoming freshman class, "Look to your left and look to your right. One of you will not be here at the end of the semester." During his four years at U of I, Ryan worked very hard, and at times, he really struggled. Many nights he stayed up to pore over his books. Many weekends he gave up parties and the chance to come home. I never had to tell him what to do. I could always count on Ryan to meet his own expectation of himself. He finished the extremely challenging EE program in four years, a remarkable achievement, as most students took five years to complete the undergraduate program.

I always knew that the time I had with my children at home would pass by quickly. I knew that my kids would grow up too fast and leave too soon. Raising my children was one of the most rewarding experiences in my life. I was blessed with so many happy memories of watching them grow, and I hung on to the joy of having them around for as long as I could.

Ryan graduated during the golden years of telecommunications. Jobs for EE graduates were plentiful. Companies competed to hire the best and brightest. Salary offers were record-high and often came with signing bonuses.

Ryan had more than four job offers when he graduated from UIUC. They included big names such as Nokia, Lucent, and AT&T. Ryan signed on with Motorola even though it wasn't the top offer financially. During the two summer internships he worked at Motorola (he was hired without any help from me), he developed a true affection for the company. I was proud that he chose to join the company that I had called home for over twenty years, and I was ecstatic that he would be staying around the Chicago area.

When Ryan graduated from college and found a good job, I knew it wouldn't be long before he would be leaving the nest. He stayed with me for exactly one year, saving as much money as he could for a down payment towards a house. At age twenty-two, Ryan decided that he was ready to buy his own place.

Like most of his friends, Ryan wanted to live in downtown Chicago rather than in the suburbs. The daily commute from Chicago to Motorola's headquarters in Schaumburg would be a painful thirty-plus miles. The commute time could easily take more than one hour depending on the traffic. But that didn't faze Ryan. The real estate market was hot, and condos in downtown Chicago were selling like hotcakes. After a very short search, Ryan made his decision to purchase a one-bedroom one-bath condo in a Chicago neighborhood called Lakeview.

Ryan bought that condo without one dime of help from me. I had taught him fiscal responsibility and self-reliance. He proved to me that he had learned those values well. I was honored when Ryan asked me to accompany him to his closing. I was bursting with pride when the realtor handed him the keys.

Megan, Clark, and I helped Ryan moved into his first place and we helped with the painting of the walls, but everything else was all Ryan. He bought furniture from Marshall Fields and Ikea. He put his own decorating touches on the walls and floors and created a cozy bachelor's pad. He was so proud to be a homeowner.

But it wasn't all work and no play. Ryan had a ton of friends, and most of them lived in the city. These twentysomethings all had good jobs, nice apartments, and nice cars. On any given weekend, there would be a party, a get-together to play video games, a meet-up at some nice restaurant or bar, or plans to attend a game of baseball or football.

Ryan's friends were a mix of high school and college friends. He had a very tight-knit group of friends in high school, which expanded into an even larger group of friends in college. There were romances that crisscrossed these relationships, so much so that the group got even larger as time went on. Maybe it was the loneliness and isolation of our family in his childhood that drove Ryan to seek out a large family of friends. I was thrilled that he had found more brothers and sisters than I could give him.

Ryan and Hilary's relationship was the result of one of those college and high school connections. A couple of weeks into the first semester at U of I, his high school friend Erica invited Ryan to go rollerblading with her and her new friend Hilary from her dorm floor. Ryan was smitten. Hilary, a blue-eyed, brown-haired beauty with the sunniest of smiles, was from Cincinnati. A few weeks later, when Ryan mentioned Hilary to Megan, he made this revelation: "This is the girl I'm going to marry."

Ten years after they met in college, Ryan and Hilary announced their engagement. When I got the news, I was all choked up. The lyrics from the song "Sunrise, Sunset" from *Fiddler on the Roof* rang in my head. "Is this the little girl I carried? Is this the little boy at play? I don't remember growing older. When did they?"

On a warm, breezy autumn day in October of 2006, on a beautiful hilltop venue overlooking the city of Cincinnati, I watched Ryan married the love of his life. There he was, my little boy, all grown up. *When did he get to be so tall?* I watched as he played host to all the friends and relatives who came to take part in his joyous occasion. His handsome face was beaming. He smiled broadly, and his voice was firm but tender as he and Hilary exchanged their wedding vows. I felt proud, and a little sad. Of course, I was happy to see my son reach this joyous milestone in his life. This is what every mother wants for her child. But wistfully, I mused, *where did the years go?*

For the mother-and-son dance at the reception, the DJ played "You Raise Me Up." The beautiful Josh Groban lyrics spoke of love, strength and gratitude—a heartfelt message as if spoken by Ryan himself. There is no greater reward for a mother than her son's expression of love and gratitude at his own wedding. It was a magnificent moment when Ryan gave me a final twirl around the dance floor as the last notes of the song played.

Ryan's wedding brought an unexpected gift of a family reunion. I hadn't seen my brother Charlie's family since I visited one time in London while traveling for work. My nephew and niece, Kelvin and Katherine, were teenagers then. Now, almost fifteen years later, I learned that they were planning to come to the wedding. Furthermore, Kelvin had a girlfriend named Emily. I quickly responded that we would be delighted to have them come. And yes, Emily must come. The cousins, who had only met twice as children, would be meeting for the first time as adults.

The reunion was the icing on the cake that marked a perfect wedding. Even though the visit was brief and the circumstance hectic, we got to know each other as family for the first time. I was struck by the realization that these children had grown up in London with very little family just like my children. And yet to their credit they had grown into strong, loving, and accomplished people. As the wedding celebration came to a close, friends and family formed a circle holding each other shoulder to shoulder and swaying to "Bless the Broken Road" by Rascal Flatts. As we joined our voices to the lyrics exalting God's plan that led us to each other in spite of the broken, crooked path, emotions filled the room. This is what family is all about. This is what love is all about.

Two years later Ryan and Hilary would travel with Clark and me to Hong Kong to attend Kelvin and Emily's wedding. It would be the first time that Ryan came home with me as an adult. It would the first time that Hilary set foot in my birthplace in Macau. It would be the last time I saw my mother.

37

The Longest Year

THE YEAR WAS 2009. It was going to be a big year. Megan was getting married in July. I would turn sixty in September. Ryan and Hilary were expecting their first child, a daughter, in October.

On the 4th of July, as the nation celebrated its birthday, Megan exchanged wedding vows with her high school sweetheart, Jon. It was the culmination of a ten-year romance. Jon and Megan met during their sophomore year in high school and had been together ever since. In their high school yearbook, they were named "the most likely couple to get married," and that had proved to be true. Now, ten years later, Megan a high school teacher and Jon a firefighter, were ready to walk down the aisle and make a lifetime commitment to each other.

In a time-honored tradition, Megan asked me to accompany her to look for her wedding dress. I was ecstatic. We made it our special mother-daughter date. On the third of such dates, we found the dress. Megan picked a strapless ivory gown with a softly beaded and ruche bodice sewn at a slight slant. It was whimsical yet simple and elegant. It suited her perfectly. A thousand emotions swelled in me when I saw her try on her wedding dress for the first time. My little girl was getting married. She would go from my house to her husband's house. Even though she was twenty-six years old, she was still my baby. It was hard to prepare myself to let her go.

On the day of her wedding, Megan was a radiant bride. She wore her hair swept to one side adorned with white orchids. The pink and purple orchids she picked as the motif for her wedding accentuated the exotic beauty that epitomized my daughter inside and out. If I wondered what her new family thought of her, it was answered by an unexpected performance at the reception. Her father-in-law wrote a song for the new couple taking a line that Megan liked to use, "That's just the way it is," serenading her on the guitar along with Jon's younger brother Michael. Jason, Jon's older brother, read a poem that Jon wrote when he first met Megan, calling her the vision of an angel.

As the night's celebration went on, there was another surprise. Jon announced to the wedding guests that he couldn't have his new bride miss the fireworks on the 4th of July, so he had ordered a special performance of fireworks for her at the balcony overlooking the golf course. It was a spectacular show. I felt such joy for my daughter and such comfort as her mother knowing that her new family loved her so much. The fireworks were also a befitting sign that they would always have fireworks in their marriage.

My job as a mother was done. I had raised two wonderful children and watched them grow into happy, strong, and loving individuals. They had come into their own and taken their rightful place in society. I felt so proud. "Go ahead and take a bow," I told myself. Raising my children was truly the most rewarding job I ever had!

In September, I turned sixty. Although I loved throwing parties for others, most of my own birthdays were low-key because I didn't really enjoy the attention. So it was a huge surprise when I walked into our favorite weekend spot called the Dover Straits for what I thought was going to be a small quiet dinner with Clark, Ryan, and Hilary, and saw over twenty of our closest friends and relatives sitting in the back of the lounge shouting "Surprise!" Even my stepdaughter Christine had flown in from Denver to join in the celebration. It was the perfect birthday party. The food was great, the wine and beer were flowing, and everyone joined on the dance floor. I couldn't have had a better sixtieth birthday!

As October rolled by, Ryan and Hilary began to get ready for the baby's arrival. On the evening of October 13, we got the call that Hilary had gone into labor. Clark and I hurried to the hospital to wait for the baby's birth. Shortly after midnight on October 14, Avery Nicole was born. Clark and I met Avery a couple of hours later. She was beautiful and perfect. My son is now a father!

Turning sixty scared me. How did I get here? Getting old took me by surprise. I had been so busy with raising children, making a living, building my career, and boom! Here I am, an early retirement candidate. AARP kept peppering me with incentives to join. Invitations to retirement planning seminars clogged my mailbox. People told me I looked a lot younger than my age. Good genes for sure, but I was feeling the unmistakable pain at the joints, the crackling sound when I bent my knees, the blood pressure and cholesterol issues ... My daily regimen of Silver Centrum, blood thinning aspirin, and Caltrate twice a day were reminders that I had entered a new stage in my life.

Inside I was screaming, *No, I am not old!* Nothing inside me has changed. The person in my heart and in my brain is still the same. I still have the fire in my belly and the conviction that I can do anything I put my mind to. I still wake up in the morning and look forward to the day with purpose and determination to tackle whatever comes my way. So why does this age thing hang over me like a cloud? Why do I feel like I am not sup-posed to plan and reach for the stars as I did years ago? Why does my age make me feel like I am approaching some kind of an expiration date?

Slowly I learned to accept my age as a gift. Throughout the years, I willed myself into adopting a "can-do" attitude because I needed my job to be able to provide for my children. Now my job is no longer the driving force in my life. I am learning to focus on myself. I have learned how im-portant it is to exercise, diet, and stay healthy. I have found my stride and I have learned to appreciate the pleasures of everyday things—taking a long walk with my husband, seeing a good movie, enjoying a delicious meal, learning a new dance step. I am becoming keenly aware that time is pre-cious, and I want to make sure that my days ahead will be quality days: physically, mentally, and emotionally.

Just when I thought I had a perfect year in 2009, life dealt me an un-expected blow. On December 10, I received a call from my sister Amy in Hong Kong. My mother had been taken to the hospital. She had contracted a horrible condition called Toxic Epidermal Necrolysis as the result of tak-ing an over-the-counter cold pill. A reaction to medication was causing the skin to blister and to peel off her body. It had a mortality rate of 30 to 40 percent, but that was much higher for older people. My mother had lost over 30 percent of her skin and was being treated like a burn victim. I was devastated and petrified.

My mother had a long history of allergic reactions to medication. This same condition had happened to her twenty years ago. She was hospitalized for six weeks and finally pulled through. It was one of the most horrific experiences of her life. Since then we kept a long list of medications that she must avoid. On the day of this incident, the maid Ah-Hing had pur-chased a cold pill for my mother. The key ingredient in the cold pill was a medication that topped the checklist of my mother's forbidden medications.

Why did Ah-Hing ignore my family's repeated instructions to check with the doctor before giving my mother any foreign medication? It could be carelessness. It could be that like many people, she didn't think allergic reactions were real. She probably thought that we over-exaggerated my mother's medical condition. We would never find out why this horrible ac-cident happened, but it did.

Throughout this time, I asked Amy, "Should I come home?"

"Mother said no," Amy told me. "Mother said to tell you that there is no need. It will take time, but she will be all right."

Even though my mother was suffering excruciating pain from the peeling skin, I think she really believed that she would eventually pull through like she did the last time.

Two days later my sister called and told me that my mother had been moved to the ICU. One day after that, the news came that she had devel-oped infections. Her platelets were extremely low and so was her blood pressure. Even the strongest medication couldn't help to raise her blood pressure to an acceptable level. She was placed on a respiratory machine because she could no longer breathe on her own. I immediately booked my ticket to go home.

On Sunday evening, December 13, I took the family out for dinner. It was the night before I was to leave for Macau. Megan's birthday was coming up in a few days. I wanted to celebrate it early, as I would be in Macau on her birthday.

At 7:30 p.m., my phone rang. I knew it was Amy because my cell phone registered "Private Call" the way it did whenever I got an international call. *Amy is just calling to confirm my itinerary for tomorrow*, I thought. Nothing prepared me for the tormented voice of my sister at the other end of the line. "Our mother is gone," she sobbed. All I could hear coming out of my mouth was "No! No! No!" I was hysterical. I couldn't stop screaming.

My mother was gone. I would never be able to call her in the morning as I did most Thursdays before I started work. I would never again hear her voice on the other end of the line. I recalled one of our last conversations.

"Mom, how are you? What did you have for dinner today? How is the weather? Have you been exercising?"

"What's there to eat?!" she complained as she always did. "The doctor said I can't have too much rice or bread because of my diabetes. I only ate a fistful of rice for dinner. I'm not allowed to have any sweets. It's too hot to walk. But I walk in the apartment. I walked five hundred steps today." She giggled. She knew she was lying.

"Are you sure you walked five hundred steps? How many times did you walk from the living room to your bedroom?"

"Twice." Again she giggled. She knew that was not five hundred steps.

"You've got to try harder." I said. "If you don't use your legs, you won't be able to walk in the years to come." I tried to be stern with her, but I knew it would be of no use. My mother didn't like to exercise. We were just rehashing the same stuff to make small talk.

"Okay, I will try." My mother laughed. "Now let's talk about you. How have you been?"

At the end of every call she would say, "Thank you for calling. You made me so happy!"

My mother was gone. I would no longer hear her voice. I would never again see her smile.

My mother was my biggest fan. "You look good in this. You should keep it." She always insisted that I take anything I liked from her wardrobe—a new sweater she was given, a new pair of shoes she had bought, a new bag someone gave her for her birthday. Her love for us was unconditional. From her I learned to do the same for my own children.

What is it like to no longer have parents? Does that make me an orphan? How will I feel when I go home again? Macau will no longer be my home. When I come back, I will be a visitor like millions of other visitors to Macau. Next time I return to Macau, my parents' apartment will be sold. I will no longer have a home to go to. Macau will never be the same to me again.

Clark and I made the trip to Macau that I never wanted to make. All the children came to the funeral, even my brother Charlie whom I had not seen for over twenty-five years. For the first time since 1964, all five of us siblings were together. We had all visited over the years, but never together. It was so sad that my mother never had the chance to see all of her children together for the past forty years. It would have made her so happy.

Making the funeral arrangements was difficult, but going through my mother's apartment afterwards was twice as hard. Mainly we divided up the old photos. We also went back to the house where we were born and reminisced about the time when we were children. So many memories; so great the sadness.

Amy's maid, Marion who was at the hospital helping with my mother's care during her final hours, shared with me this heartbreaking detail:

Before my mother went into the ICU, she said to the nurse, "I will miss my daughter and she will miss me."

"What is the name of your daughter?" the nurse asked.

"Her name is Joanna." My mother was never conscious again after she went into the ICU. I was comforted knowing that I was in her thoughts in her final hours, but I was overwhelmed with sorrow that I never had the chance to say goodbye.

My mother was buried next to my father on December 19. A visitation and memorial service was held at the funeral home the night before the funeral. The memorial service was conducted by Chi Do Tong, our family's parish church where my mother had all of us baptized. The church choir was present. The service was solemn and respectful, honoring my mother as a devout church member and reassuring the family that she was now with her heavenly father. My mother would have been pleased.

At the memorial service, the pastor asked if any of the children would care to say something about our mother. Amy and I spoke. Amy spoke emotionally about her childhood memories of my mother and all the things that my mother had taught her, including how to sing English songs when she was little. Then it was my turn.

I spoke in my broken Cantonese. I spoke of my mother's accomplishments, her devotion as a Christian, and the sacrifices she made as a mother. But most of all, I wanted to say out loud what my mother meant to me.

"Many people said that I looked like my mother. For the rest of my life I will have to work hard to learn to *be* like my mother— her gentleness, her patience, her compassion. It will take me a lifetime, but I am going to honor my mother by trying to be more like her in all that I do."

"Mother, I will forever miss you. I hope I will see you again."

Before we all parted ways after the wake, the five of us took a group picture in the ceremonial hall. Later I was shocked to see how the picture had turned out. There standing in front of the framed portrait of our mother were the five of us, starting with Amy and ending with Jimmy. We were standing in our birth order! It was as if our mother had reached down and arranged us in the way that she had brought us into this world. The five of us have not been together in one place for forty-five years. Perhaps it was the way that she wanted to see us again.

In the months after my mother passed away, I was so overcome with grief that I sat down and painstakingly created a digital photo album entitled

The Ng Family Album. The album chronicled in photos my family's story from my parents' youth to their marriage, the family they raised, and all the major milestones such as weddings and births. It was a bittersweet documentary celebrating the joys of a family's saga. I did it as a tribute to my parents. I want to document in perpetuity their remarkable lives and our journey as a family.

The same day my mother was buried, my nephew's (Amy's son) wife gave birth to a baby boy they named Chat-Fong, the first great-grandson whom my mother would never meet. How amazing is the circle of life!

38

A New Chapter

SO THE NEXT generation had arrived. With the birth of my grand-daughter Avery and my grandnephew Chat-Fong, a new chapter for our family had begun. We bid farewell to 2009 and said hello to a new decade. I was stepping into a new era as a person with no living parents but also as a first-time grandparent. The emotions were bittersweet.

There is a beginning and an end to everything. It was no different with my job. After a long and successful tenure at Motorola, my run came to a close.

On April 6, 2011, I was called into my manager's office for a "quick chat." He had a serious look on his face. The Human Resource manager came in five minutes later and I knew what was about to happen. My job as Director of Business Development, Advanced Services, had been elimi-nated. I was given a severance package that included six month's salary and other medical and outplacement services.

The news was not a complete shock. My seniority and my compensa-tion made me a huge downsizing target. The company had shrunk so much that the number of senior level jobs had also dropped dramatically as a re-sult. Young, innovative minds fresh out of college who would work for a lot less were a better fit for the times. The Chinese have a saying: "In an advancing river, the waves from behind push the ones ahead of them." It was time to make room for the next generation of workers.

I was fortunate to have been with Motorola through its glory days. Motorola had enjoyed an unprecedented rise to the top of the wireless communications world in the 1990s and multiple rounds of remarkable comebacks, but in the past decade, the company had gone through increasingly hard times. During the past five years, besieged by competition from the iPhone and other smart-phone manufacturers, the company was struggling to stay in the game. Carl Icahn had goaded the company for years into splitting into two entities in order to return value to the stockholders. He finally succeeded. On June 2010, Motorola filed Form 10-K with the United States Securities and Exchange Commission to split into two companies: Motorola Mobility (mobile phone) and Motorola Solutions (enterprise and government communications).

In the process of the separation, many more lost their jobs. Miraculously I managed to survive the massive restructuring and landed in Motorola Solutions. The company that I joined was much smaller than the one I started with. The new company employed less than twenty-five thousand, a far cry from the ninety-five thousand when I joined, not to mention the hundred and forty-seven thousand Motorola once employed in its heyday. Motorola Solutions was focused on the government and public safety communications business. It would be back to the beginning. Motorola had come full circle.

Richard M. Daley retired from office as Chicago's mayor on May 6 after an illustrious twenty-two year run. He said goodbye with a fifty-ward farewell tour. Talk show hostess Oprah Winfrey closed her iconic twenty-five year *Oprah* show on May 25 with a double-episode extravaganza. I was in good company when I retired in June 2011, one month after Mayor Daley and Oprah left their beloved jobs. I had joined Motorola on July 14, 1980; my last day with Motorola was June 17, 2011. I had worked for Motorola for thirty-one years, or half of my age of almost sixty-two. I left Motorola without any fanfare.

Clark and I went on a Baltic Cruise for our eighth wedding anniversary. We returned on June 15. Two days later, I turned in my Motorola badge. After my exit interview, I stopped by to see Ryan. He insisted that he would walk me out. As I walked out of the building, Ryan paused to take a photo. Later he posted the picture for the family to see.

"Here's Mom leaving Moto one last time. Thanks for letting me walk you out, Mom. You did a fantastic job and will be missed here. But the best is yet to come for you! We love you!"

How do you leave a job after thirty-one years? Working for Motorola had become an old habit, a way of life for me. For thirty years, I woke up in the morning and walked into a familiar building with the Batwings logo. Over the years some things had changed—the floor layouts, the artwork in the hallways, and even the color of the batwings—but the familiar campus, the view from the windows, the smell of the cafeteria, and the echo in the meeting rooms had become fixtures in my mind.

Leaving Motorola was like leaving home for good. I raised my family while working for Motorola. My children came here for the annual *Easter Egg Hunt* and *Take Your Children to Work* events. It was not too long ago that I was flying all over the world, taking on all kinds of new challenges, and working all kinds of hours. I was on a hamster wheel that kept on going until someone pushed a button and brought it to a jolting halt. Where do I go from here? What will I do when I wake up in the morning? How will I find my purpose again? Will I feel worthless, bored, depressed?

It sounds like a cliché, but things do happen for a reason. After I left Motorola, I was able to spend time finishing my memoir. As I wrote this book, it took me back to my childhood and my early years as an immigrant, and a light switch was flipped on.

I began to see my past in a new light. Never before had I thought of Macau as an exotic, beloved, and beautiful place. I didn't appreciate the physical charm, the history, and the cultural and architectural richness of my birthplace. Born in a colony, I was raised as a citizen of no country, with no sense of affinity or allegiance to any sovereignty or ethnicity. I was not proud of my Chinese heritage and my humble beginnings in Macau. Along the way, a door had been opened. I saw myself standing shoulder to shoulder with a people of strength, resilience, and the uncompromising will to survive and succeed. I am so proud to be Chinese and to have inherited the Chinese values of hard work and excellence, respect for parents, love for family, and honor and pride in myself. I want so much to pass on to the next generation the Chinese traditions, wisdoms, and philosophies that have sustained me throughout my life journey.

When I became a U.S. citizen, I didn't know how to embrace the country that had embraced me. America, my adopted country, had welcomed me from day one with open arms. It never asked anything of me except to take advantage of the tremendous opportunities that came my way. The America I came to know was not a country paved with gold. It's a country with a big heart that offers hope and the permission to dream larger-than-life dreams. I discovered that the American dream is not an entitlement. It's the freedom to be different and a place where we can work hard to make our lives into anything we want them to be. The right to "life, liberty and the pursuit of happiness" in the American Declaration of Independence is not a platitude; it is a call to action to find fulfillment within ourselves. Happiness is all up to me. I learned to give myself permission to love and be loved, to make the most of every day, and to laugh out loud and live out loud.

Professionally, I dismissed the amazing career I had built as one of luck and necessity. I saw my job as simply the means to an end—that of providing for my family. As I look back, I am in awe of what my professional journey has given me—a lasting gift of self-respect and personal growth, and the opportunity to realize my potential. It was a privilege to have been associated with Motorola—a company that built its reputation on strong business ethics, quality, and innovation. As a woman, I am humbled to have been part of the revolution of the 1970s and 1980s when the first generation of American moms started to go to work in corporate America. I am honored to be one of many who broke down racial and gender barriers in the workplace and put an Asian female face on the pages of the American corporate journal. I hope that the trail we blazed has helped to open doors for the next generation.

What a dazzling story I discovered when I put into words the story of my childhood! Woven into the tapestry of time are the rich colors of culture, tradition, sacrifice, survival, and triumph. I feel privileged to be the teller of the story of my family. This book is a tribute to my parents, who gave us everything they could so that we can have the life we enjoy today.

I didn't realize how remarkable my journey has been until I put pen to paper. Through the process of writing my story, I found who I am. I came away with a strong sense of myself, and I found great pride in where I came from and the journey I have taken.

Perhaps there is another chapter in my book still to be written. But I finally understood the wisdom of *The Old Farmer Who Lost His Horse*. I have found contentment, happiness, and balance. I consider myself very fortunate, but I also know that I make my own luck. I learn that when one door closes, it is within my power to open another. I am aware of how fragile and fleeting our lives are. All worldly fortunes—money, fame, status, power—they don't last. In the end, what prevail are the relationships we build along the way. The people who take the journey with us, who love and support us and cheer us on—they are the enduring wealth that we carry with us.

I am not ready to write the Epilogue of my life, but if I could pass a message to my children and grandchildren, this is the message:

I hope that my life inspires you to embrace every opportunity that comes along, to get out and see the world, to live life fully, to love intensely, and to never be afraid to take chances.

The aromatic skies of Macau beckoned me to take a chance on life. I did and discovered its endless possibilities.

Ryan said it well. Maybe the best is yet to come.

39

What Happens Now?

I WOKE UP this morning at 5:30 a.m. I still haven't quite mastered the art of sleeping in, even though my time is no longer bound by office hours, due dates, schedules and meetings.

The dawning sky over Lake Michigan is a photographic masterpiece. Streaks of burnt orange and metallic gold fill the canvas of my front windows. Our Chicago condo is our weekend get-away. We come here every Friday evening to nest as only empty-nesters can.

Five years ago, Clark and I decided to buy a downtown place. It sounds ungracious, but without the responsibilities of child rearing, our suburban home has become, dare I say, somewhat boring and lonesome. Both Clark and I are city people. We know that living in Chicago would make us feel that we are in the middle of something special, not to mention the best way to enjoy Chicago's many entertainment, cultural and culinary pleasures.

Clark is still sleeping. I sit on the windowsill and sip my perfect cup of morning Nespresso coffee. Our high-rise condo apartment sits on Lake Shore Drive in front of the iconic Chicago landmark—the Navy Pier. It is late August 2012, and the weatherman has forecasted another warm and humid 90-degree Chicago summer day. In the distance, the blue waters of Lake Michigan are twinkling in the morning sunlight. Navy Pier is empty; the Ferris-Wheel perches motionless between the pillars of the majestic dome at the end of the pier. To the left of our building, a man on a riding machine is raking the sands of Ohio Street Beach into perfect concentric circles, as if doing the work of a Zen Buddhist monk. A handful of early-riser runners and devoted dog-walkers speckle the concrete-paved walkway along the shoreline. Hundreds of Seagulls roost inaudibly on top of the wreckage of the old pier. A soothing peace washes over me. I love watching the lake from the windows of our twenty-third-floor apartment.

It has been exactly one year since I retired. Still I can't get used to the word "retired." How I dislike that word! It makes me sound useless, defunct, obsolete.

The Chinese have a saying "Falling leaves return to their roots." It rather explains why I felt the urge to travel back to my past after I stopped working. In September, Clark and I took the 40-minute drive to Barat College. I have only visited my Alma Mata once since I graduated. The college had closed down a few years ago when it became financially insolvent. A chain-link fence had been built to stop trespassers. The campus site was up for sale. Clark took pictures of me in front of the Old Main building. Memories of my first arrival in America rushed back and I was overcome with nostalgia. Clark then drove me to downtown Lake Forest and to the Deerpath Inn. The establishment had changed hands over the years and the Inn was no longer a residence house, although it had retained glimmers of its old-world past. Still a fine-dining destination, the Deerpath Inn now catered to the more casual American palate. The original English Pub—the Hunt Room—now housed a Sushi bar. We ate dinner at the main Dining room. A huge prosciutto-slicing machine mounted with a whole leg of ham sat ostentatiously in the middle of the dining room, reminding its diners of the Inn's opulent European past. In the shadows of the massive chandeliers that still graced the dining room, I saw the skinny weary-eyed nineteen-year-old Chinese girl walking up to our table with the fully stacked dinner tray, ready to be served. I was back in 1969 with the memories of my first job in America. Nobody I knew still worked here any more.

In February I made my trip to Macau for the first time since my mother died, not counting the funeral trip. Actually, Clark and I also went to Manila, Shenzhen and Hong Kong. But the focus for me was always Macau. I was part looking forward and part dreading the visit. I'll be visiting my parents' grave for the first time after the tombstone has been "updated" with my mother's particulars. The visit was emotional. It was as if I had been saving all the tears so that they could empty out of me like the waters of Niagara Falls when I see my mother again. But I could never see my mother again. This, her resting place, will be the only place that I could visit her now. I still can't speak about my mother without choking up with tears.

I have been sitting on the windowsill for an hour. The sky has slowly turned a pale shade of dusty pink and blue. I take another sip of my coffee and kick into planning mode: *What will we do today?* This morning we will take a long walk along the winding Chicago River with its many historic bridges. Later today, Clark and I will walk down to Navy Pier and see which bands are playing at the Beer Garden. Maybe we will listen to a pseudo-Jimmy Buffet performance and dance to *Brown Eye Girl*. More likely, it will be a pop/rock band playing Carly Rae Jepsen's *Call Me Maybe*. No matter if it's Rock, Jazz, Pop, Country, or Latin music, all the same we'll enjoy tapping our toes to the infectious music. Before Navy Pier goes to sleep, fireworks will light up the sky at precisely 10:15 p.m. After that, we'll take our 5-minute walk home, which inevitably turns into 15 minutes depending on the size of the crowd that empty out of the pier.

Or maybe we'll do a completely different version of the day. We may take our ravenous morning appetite downstairs to our favorite gourmet grocery store/café called *Fox and Obel* and have Lox and Bagel for breakfast. It only takes a couple of dollars and less than 15 minutes to hop on a Water Taxi to the Planetarium or to the Field Museum. Or maybe we'll stroll to Buckingham Fountain or walk to the famous Cloud Gate at Millennium Park and watch the tourists take endless photos of their reflections in *The Bean*. Or if the Magnificent Mile beckons, we'll go window-shopping on Chicago's Champs Elysées—Michigan Avenue—and see what's the latest trends in upscale stores like Prada, Chanel, and Tiffany's. And how about trying that Korean BBQ place that just opened up on Ohio Street? Too early to turn in for the day, we may walk a block to the AMC Theatre to watch the newly opened Bourne action movie before midnight.

Chicago is an exciting city with personality to spare. It has a perfect combination of style and glitz, character and glamour. In Chicago, we live like two hip, carefree twentysomethings without the worry of money or kids. Our city life is thrilling. We always look forward to our weekends.

During the weekdays however, I'm finding that I am still an apprentice to this thing called *retirement*. It seems that I still have the need to fill all the nooks and crannies of my time. My hardcore work ethic has its downside: pure pleasure is not in my vocabulary. How do I purge feelings of guilt when I am not doing anything that could be remotely labeled as "productive"? What's the difference between being bored out of my mind and quietly enjoying the leisure of doing nothing?

Now that I have time to do anything I want, suddenly I have no clue what I want to do. My sister Amy (the retired lawyer) once told me that after so many years in a high stress career, when she retires she would take a mindless job like—becoming a cashier at a grocery store. *Hello, how are you? Twenty-five dollars and twenty cents please. Have a nice day!* That never happened. She is too busy babysitting her grandchildren. My friend Lynn told me that when she retires from her mind-numbing accounting job she would work in a bakery and bake mouth-watering breads and cakes all day long. She is retired and has gained so much weight that the last thing she needs to do is to work in a bakery.

The first year of my retirement was typical of so many people's first year of retirement. I tackled all the projects I never got around to doing: organize photos, clean out closets, and travel to every long-anticipated venue until I was dizzy from traveling. And then all is quiet. Clark goes back to work and I'm home alone. So *what happens now?*

Think, Joanna, think. What do you want to do now? Do you want to write, travel, learn to speak Mandarin, do volunteer work? I thought you want to have time to pursue what you love—writing, so do it!

I feel a hand gently touching my shoulder. It's Clark. He is smiling at me with such tenderness.

"Jo-sen (Good Morning), darling."

"How did you sleep?"

"Okay."

"Just Okay? Dreaming too much again?"

"Yeah, I don't know why." I smiled back at him.

He kissed me on the top of my head, just like the first time he kissed me.

"It's all right. You can take a nap later if you want."

Why can't I sleep like a baby now that I have no more practical worries? My perfect triangle of career, motherhood and marriage is complete. What is still making me so restless?

Life is a circle. You are never done. The human spirit yearns to grow, learn, and evolve. It needs to be jolted by emotional and physical experiences in order to be reminded that it's alive.

I need to find a beautiful wild horse to tame again. What's different this time is that it'll be a horse that I choose to ride. I'll take my time and enjoy the experience. I'll be careful that it doesn't throw me off and break my legs. What I need is a new challenge—something difficult, something that takes a lot of time, something that takes patience to learn and to master, something that I never thought I could be good at.

Maybe I'll finally learn to play golf.

The End

Acknowledgements

I always knew that I wanted to write this book. But now I know with certainty that this book would never have been published had it not been for the special people in my life.

My greatest debt of gratitude goes to my husband Clark, who is my rock. He refused to allow me to be content with this book being an unpublished project. It is his love and his faith in me that cradled me through the ups-and-downs of this journey and thrust me over the goal-line.

I especially want to thank my friend Bruce Briley, an author himself, for giving me that much-needed shot-in-the-arm when he convinced me that my book is literary-worthy, and, "Don't you deprive the world of it."

I am indebted to Diana Finch for helping me find the title that resonates with my story arc.

A heartfelt Thank-You goes to Wei Feng, who read the entire manuscript in two days, and showed me that my story can touch lives, because she told me it changed hers.

Several people read early drafts of the manuscript, each offering a particular perspective. Their insightful comments helped immeasurably, and so too, did their encouragement and support. I thank Mary Jo and John Bennett, Ed and Judy Boduch, Marilyn Webb, Linda Gunn, Janice Urban, Sandy Bachman, Chuck Powers, Janiece Webb, and my dearest friend Joanne Finer.

To my uncle Say Kau Fu, my mother's only living sibling, I send my fondest Thank-You. We didn't know very much about each other's lives before he read my manuscript. It meant so much to me when he told me that my book had the potential of becoming a best-seller, and, "As your uncle, I am tremendously proud of you." In his words, I heard the voice of my mother cheering me on.

I want to thank my family, who unwittingly became characters in my book. My children Ryan and Megan, my parents, and my siblings—all of whom, in their own ways inspired me, and subconsciously contributed to the content of this book. They have nothing to gain by this book, only their love to support me in all that I do.

Last but not least, I wish to thank my amazing publisher and friend Steve Jackson and the wonderful and talented staff at Telemachus Press. They are the best partners I could ask for in my maiden voyage as an author.

About the Author

Joanna Ng was born and raised in the Chinese-Portuguese colony of Macau in South-East Asia. She came to the United States at nineteen to attend Barat College in Lake Forest, Illinois in 1969. She was hired by Motorola in 1980 and worked in the telecommunications industry for over thirty years until she retired in 2011. Joanna is now focusing on a writing career. She lives in Chicago with her husband Clark.